**INTRODUCTION BY
DOUGLAS RUSHKOFF**

22
IDEAS
ABOUT
THE
FUTURE

**EDITED BY
BENJAMIN GREENAWAY & STEPHEN ORAM**

Print Edition
ISBN: 978-1-7395939-0-2
Published by Cybersalon 2022

Cover design by Jessica Bell
Interior design by Amie McCracken

This collection of provocations from the think tank Cybersalon brings together a blend of near-future speculative fiction and non-fiction commentary from leading experts in the fields of health, community, retail, and money. Together, they shine a light behind the cornerstones of our lives to reveal the unexpected and invite you to cast your critical eye on technology and its effect on society. Be prepared for warnings and inspirations from those who speculate about the future and those who make it a reality.

Contents

PART 4: The Digitisation of Central Money

Preface

OUR FUTURE will be more complex than we expected. Instead of flying cars we got night-vision killer drones and automated elderly care with geolocation surveillance bracelets to track grandma. In this book we take a different approach to interrogating the future and the impact of networked technologies on our neighbourhood communities, health care, how we shop, and how we manage our money. For thousands of years humans passed on their warnings about risks and dangers to their societies via oral stories. Here we have chosen the medium of near-future stories to pass on our learnings from a twelve-month research programme, as well as from the many previous years of Cybersalon's investigation into the data-driven society and our networked lives.

The rapid acceleration of our journey into a fully data-driven society has caught our civilisation unprepared. Over the last five years, the cost of scraping millions of intimate, personal data points from social media has dropped to the cost of a sandwich. The cloud storage costs of terabytes of data points on our lives have fallen to near zero. Reading data and finding the right triggers for each of us has been made easy by artificial intelligence, which constantly sieves through our individual data and susses out quickly what makes us buy, vote for a political party, or even select a life partner. We are no longer in control of those choices, as they are now in the hands of big technology companies with massive processing power and little ethical regulation. The stories in this book offer a lens through which to spot the onslaught on our free will and lessons on how to notice where our personal decisions are subverted to respond to automated triggers. They will also show the areas where new technologies can offer some glimpses of hope and new opportunities.

Third-party cookies have become the bane of our everyday networked lives. If you casually browse new bikes online, a moment later every social media site you visit is filled to the brim with ads for new bikes. Allowing these was arguably one of the worst governance decisions made about the Internet and it spurred us to form Cybersalon as a think tank to fight against the impact of this 24/7 surveillance, to regain the dignity of online life, and to push back against the data free-for-all and dataholic tech giants.

Little did we know that the risk was not just the big tech companies making millions from our data, but also how we, as humans, respond to advertising bots appealing to our subconsciouses. The impact is our uncontrolled, sub-rational response to personalised, individually profiled triggers. Those triggers "know" us intimately and can push our buttons, taking over the parts of the brain that are no longer under the supervision of our conscious self.

Our goal in writing the book, working with our experts, and commissioning the stories from near-future fiction writers was to help protect online users against subversion of their decisions by ad bots and digital manipulation, forcing us to change how we work, live, and feel.

This book is about raising our eyes above the levers, raising our minds above "your post was liked" or "someone likes a video you are tagged in". We aim to offer a new tool kit on how to lift our society above the mindlessness of the hollow convenience of digital life and fight back for your free will. We hope that the stories in this book will entertain you and also help you stand up to technology and become mindful of retaining our shared humanity.

In the old days, the guards of the tribe would be posted at the top of the nearest mountain, increasing the range of sight by an extra dozen kilometres. Being able to alarm the village early enough that the elders could decide action and the villagers could run away and hide their children in safety made the difference between life and death.

This book helps those who need to act as the guards on the peak of the nearby mountain for their own communities who are watching out to protect their digital villages and observing the data-scraping enemy, the AI-equipped tech giants, social media owners, and designers of dataholic pop-ups and data-scraping tools. If we can observe, we can respond, get them removed from the ecosystem, request fines, enact regulations, and also demand closure as a last resort.

Hopefully, this book demonstrates that "ethical data" is an oxymoron. It is akin to saying that ethical weapons are possible. There is no difference in using tech power to wield advantage with traditional guns, modern night-vision-equipped drones, or AI that triggers you to make choices you would not select on your own. At the end of every data capture and every data-scraping bot there is a loser and a winner. The winner is always the data scraper, rarely the data giver.

22 Ideas is a journey in time to the near-future and a climb up a few high peaks to scan the horizon for the new manipulations and attention-capture devices that loom to dehumanise us further. It is about identifying sneaky new technologies that steal our attention, and new surveillance tools that hide behind "smart care". It is also about searching for the green shoots of something useful emerging from the jungle of AI bots, something that could help networked society regain agency and control. It is about lessons for our gradual march as we learn to live alongside predatory algorithms.

What is at stake is our mindfulness, our confidence in our free will, and our ability to fight back against computers that are getting too good at understanding what makes we humans tick. It is our networked society versus the bots in the last stand for free-thinking humans. We hope the stories help you to scan the future for tech-made booby traps and inspire you to build a better, more conscious data society for us all.

Eva Pascoe.
Co-founder and Chair of Cybersalon.

Introduction

You see men sailing on their ego trip,
Blast off on their spaceship,
Million miles from reality:
No care for you, no care for me.
                    Bob Marley, "So Much Trouble in the World"

FICTION HAS always been a guilty pleasure for me. With so many urgent things going on in the real world, how dare I indulge in reading, much less writing, fiction? Don't I have a responsibility to understand and explain the realities of economic inequality, racial injustice, and climate change before engaging in fantasies of robots, space, and artificial intelligence?

Perhaps.

But after writing a couple of dozen non-fiction books and hundreds of articles, I'm not so sure that fact-based rhetoric is the best way to reach people - or even to inform them. Yes, I've gathered plenty of evidence for people who already agree with me to make their cases to others. I know many of my readers have nodded along with what I've written, feeling confirmed and vindicated by seeing their own opinions expressed for them in writing - maybe in a manner more fully formed than they've been able to articulate themselves. It's an honour and a privilege to put words to our shared sensibilities.

Still, I've become aware that no matter how well I argue, I'm painfully limited in my ability to reach through to people who don't already see the world as I do. My facts and insights don't penetrate closed minds. It's as if my premises just bounce off people's skulls and scatter on the ground, unconsidered. If only I could get people to create a sliver of an opening to suppose something new or different, even if just for a moment. If they would only consider the utterly implausible, even just for kicks, I know I could take care of the rest.

That's the beauty - the *opportunity* - of a collection like this. Speculative fiction does something very special to the otherwise closed mind. It creates space for the novel. Just allowing oneself to *pretend* that something could be true is more than enough. We can't imagine something without at least entertaining that possibility. Speculative fiction is an invitation to speculate on fictional scenarios. And in the process, we reveal truths we have hidden from ourselves.

While reality TV is busy generating dangerous fictions and creating closed-minded, racist conspiracy theorists in the process, speculative fiction exposes people to necessary truths they may never truly encounter otherwise. You can't read about the world after climate catastrophe without accepting the possibility of climate change to begin with. If you suspend your disbelief in thinking machines for long enough to follow the story of a vengeful robot, you are ready to consider the impact of autonomous vehicles on the human environment. If you allow yourself to imagine a future without debt or credit, worker or boss, hoarding or poverty, you free yourself to consider the inequalities embedded in our economic system.

But beyond the specific subjects that speculative fiction can introduce to our stubbornly rigid minds, the process of speculation itself retrains the brain. Like a form of exercise, it stretches our imaginative capacity, making our thinking more porous, flexible, and able to tolerate the surprising or absurd. Where reality addicts of all stripes can only envision a Great Awakening, apocalyptic comeuppance, or endless cycle of repression, those who embrace fiction have the freedom to eschew the inevitability of human suffering and envision alternative pathways. Ways out, ways through, or just ways. What *if?*

Speculative fiction, in particular, invites us to consider awe-inspiring new landscapes - outer space, inner space, living machines, alternative dimensions, magick sigils, and shared consciousness. And that experience of awe acts positively on the body and mind. Psychologists studying the phenomenon have found that even a brief moment of awe can help people act with an increased sense of meaning and purpose, turning our attention away from the self and toward collective self-interest. Awe even helps regulate our body's immune response and reduces inflammation - as if engendering a less defensive, aggravated response to the unknown. After a few moments of awe, people behave with greater altruism, cooperation, and self-sacrifice. It makes people feel like part of something larger than themselves.

Unlike traditional fiction, speculative fiction owes nothing to the standard, Aristotelian arc that has characterised drama and story for the past two millennia. We are used to following a male hero up the incline plane of tension into danger. He eventually reaches a crisis that requires reversal and recognition - the poison is a weapon, the talent is a flaw, the goal is the problem - then climax, catharsis, and sleep. And this same shape of striving toward a goal, up the hill, through adversity to the golden ring at the end of the journey has also characterised everything from Christianity and capitalism to Marxism and activism. We make change through ends-justifies-the-means campaigns because it's the only story architecture we know. No pain, no gain.

The best of speculative fiction frees us not only from our personal reality tunnels, but from the tired narrative conventions that limit our approaches to innovation, collaboration, consensus, and liberation. In this sense, speculative fiction is inherently revolutionary or, better, evolutionary in its purpose. Not only can things be so different, but the way in which that shift happens must also be up for discussion. Every story is a theory of change, whether or not it rises to that occasion.

Try to imagine technological innovation without the specter of a business plan or exponential growth curve. What is virtual reality or a metaverse when it's not obligated to breathe new life into a dying ticker symbol? Where else but smart sci-fi and cli-fi can we speculate on the unacknowledged externalities of these business practices and the unforeseen impacts of the technologies themselves? Imagine what technological development might look like if it weren't already sitting on top of the operating system we call corporate capitalism. Dare we?

So no, I will no longer apologise for my love of speculative and, yes, science fiction, climate fiction, cyberpunk and solar punk. In a world where nearly every experience makes us feel like we are being quantised for the benefit of an observing algorithm, we need ways of slipping between the prescribed values to the bizarre in-between spaces where life breeds and human thought mutates. Just because it's fun doesn't mean it's wrong. This is the work. This is the play.

Bob Marley was right. There is trouble in this world. Welcome to some new ones.

Douglas Rushkoff
New York, March 2022

PART 1:
The Technologisation
of Healthcare

Virtually Dead

Jule Owen

"So, YOU KNOW who I am?" Mike asked.

"Yes, of course. I saw you every day for many years. I sorted your post. You're Mr Benz."

Mike was sitting in Julian's concierge office, drinking a terrible cup of coffee and feeling grateful for it.

"So how did it happen? You being dead?" Julian asked.

"I'm not dead," Mike said.

"But you are dead. Officially."

Mike took this in, slightly stunned. After a while, he said, "It was my health plan. I had one of those watches you wear all the time and little devices they inject you with, you know? Microscopic machines that spread out in your body and measure everything in real-time?"

"I've heard of them, but I don't have health insurance. Too expensive."

Mike nodded thoughtfully, wanting to show appropriate empathy for what this implied, but really overwhelmed by his own blind panic. He continued, "The machines transmit the data back to servers in the cloud. The health insurance company owns everything. The company's tech people do some AI wizardry, analyse the data, write software to diagnose what is wrong. This software predicts outcomes, gives health advice, and automatically dispatches medicine."

Julian said, "People like me don't get access to things like that. But I've seen the adverts."

Mike continued, "The plan came with my job. As part of onboarding, a medic from the health insurance company came to my home, gave me an injection, handed me my watch, all boxed up nicely, and that was that. I forgot about it. I had always been so fit. Besides, I never had time to stop and think about my health. It was way down my list of priorities after meeting quarterly and annual targets and trying to get my bonus. There had been some alerts on my watch and emails flagging that I should log in to my dashboard. But it was near the end of the fiscal year. We were five percent off our target, and my team was working round the clock. I didn't have time to look.

"Just after the year closed, my boss scheduled a meeting with me. I thought it was to congratulate me on the numbers because we had made them after all. But when I met with him, he was with a person from HR. The HR person did all the talking. She said that the health insurance company had been in touch. I was very ill. The company would put me on sick leave, effective immediately, to concentrate on my treatment and recovery.

"The next day, a medic showed me my dashboard and explained how they got the data and the results. He said the prognosis was not great, but there was hope if I began treatment immediately. I said that I felt fine, apart from being exhausted from the push toward the year-end. He said that people often didn't realise they were sick until it was too late, and that was why their technology was so useful. A courier delivered medicine. I took it and then I felt unwell.

"At first, I couldn't cope with all the messages from colleagues wanting to know how I was. Clients sent me baskets of fruit. When the contact started to peter out, I wasn't too worried. The medic said I was responding to treatment, and there was reason to feel optimistic. In truth, I'd been burning the midnight oil and hadn't had a proper holiday in years. I spent time in my garden, going for walks, doing the exercise routine set for me by the health insurance company. Then I flatlined.

"I mean, my vitals in the health dashboard all went critical and then to zero. I rang the helpline. The person on the other end of the line was new. They promised to get someone to ring me back. No one did. It took me several days and some persistence to get anyone to talk to me.

"'That's impossible,' the health insurance executive said.

"'Well, it's not, because I am talking to you, and my dashboard says I'm dead.'"

"'If the dashboard says you're dead, you're dead. Is this a hoax?' I lost my temper, and they hung up.

"After that, everything spiralled out of control. The social media broadcasts from friends talking about their significant loss and their anger when I responded, saying that I was still alive ('Sick bastard'). Sending away the undertakers. Persuading (unsuccessfully) to stop my bank from closing my accounts. Then the bailiffs came and said that I was squatting in my cousin's apartment.

"Of course, my cousin, who is my only living blood relative, and the chief beneficiary of my will, was not going to admit to anyone who I was. My former boss, my so-called friends at work, none of them wanted anything to do with me. The health insurance company had been in touch. It was a legal matter. They were very sorry."

Mike had been talking so long he hadn't noticed Julian putting on his coat. Now he saw him slinging his bag over his shoulder.

"Sorry, Mike. I have to go. You are welcome to stay here if you like. There's a sofa in that back room. It's not so bad. I have slept on it myself."

Mike nodded. "You will help me, won't you, Julian?"

"How can I help you?"

"Tell people you know who I am."

"I did tell them. No one paid any attention. First, your cousin said she now owned your apartment, and I should give her a key.

"When I wouldn't do what she wanted, I got all these official messages from legal people. And when I still wouldn't let her in, the manager of the building came. He's my boss and let her in himself. You see, I did try, but I nearly got fired. I need this job."

After Julian left for the night, Mike sat on the sofa and looked at his watch. Everything on the screen was red.

Health Miles

Benjamin Greenaway

CONNOR HAD always said it started like a joke down the pub.

"National Health Service? More like National Sickness Service, am I right?"

An easy shot, really. Not everybody was a fan of the NHS. Not anymore. Connor, like most of his peers, had given three years of his liberty to lockdowns in the hope of saving it. So, when a popular pharmalogistics conglomerate announced a radical new recovery programme, he didn't blink. Not even at their long-standing history of labour rights convictions.

"Nothing stopping these zoonotic pandemics any time soon. And we're still paying for the last three!" he said. "Maybe it's someone else's turn to take the brunt?"

***

The programme was simple: earn rewards for healthier decisions, day by day. For simple things like drinking less alcohol, eating less fast food, and taking exercise. And thousands signed up in the first few hours. It appealed to Connor that he'd win twice over if he tried it. He was no longer in his twenties, with some shortness of breath here, an intermittent muscle ache there, and a tighter squeeze into old jeans than he was willing to admit.

It'd be good to get a little fitter, he thought. Indeed, it would be good for everyone. And a few extra treats here and there would be nice, too.

"Hello. Welcome to Implantech. Are you here to find out about the programme?"

"I am," Connor replied. He granted a share of basic contact information and the avatar connected.

"We have a wide range of rewards for your health improvements," it continued. "All courtesy of our network of sponsoring partners. Eligibility for Tier 1 begins with any qualifying evidence-gathering device. Do you currently own a programme-compatible device, Connor?"

"I think so," he replied.

The programme came in two tiers, based on the level and granularity of data gathered. It worked by assigning Improvement Points to regularly updated activity reports. For example, an improvement to your daily routine such as adding morning calisthenics, a light-to-moderate daily exercise routine, could earn credits for trips on public transport. Something more ambitious like a five-kilometre run might earn a week's upgraded media streaming, or preferential seating at a cinema or theatre.

"Tier 1 support is available for any 6G-enabled personal health monitor, exercise tracker, or location-enabled communications device. Some 5G devices are supported but may require secondary evidence validation via the Drone Surveillance Archive or your Residential Community Security feed."

"R.C.S. in my block? That'd be nice," Connor quipped.

"But my communications device is 6G. How about Tier 2?"

Improvement Points in Tier 2 were a more targeted, personal calculation and, consequently, required more detail and verification. In Tier 2 you earned a proportion of your predicted health care outcome costs – assuming you'd not been improving them with the programme. Even though it was far from a one-to-one exchange, the rewards you could earn in Tier 2 were significant.

"Aha!" warmed the salesbot. "Implantech's Tier 2 evidence gathering and validation is second to none. We are sole manufacturers of the first fully-automated monitoring and reporting solution authorised to submit claims under the Tier 2 Advanced Insight Improvement Requirements. Can I tell you about Capsule?"

The capsule device was no larger than a multivitamin yet could live in its host's digestive tract for a full month, reporting wide-spectrum biometrics, accelerometer readings, and location data to the programme twice a day.

"I've heard about that." Connor sighed, genuinely disappointed.

"As a rule, I'll never use first-generation devices on *any* platform. Feel that counts twice if it's inside me. Are there any other ways to qualify for Tier 2?" he asked, already sure of the salesbot's response.

"Improvement claims for Tier 2 can be made on your behalf by a variety of health care providers, Connor. What is the name of yours?"

"Yeah. I thought so. Sorry, but I think I'll have to pass."

Connor disconnected the feed and slouched dejectedly into his chair. "Health miles." He sighed. "As if anyone can still afford to fly."

***

The second-generation unit was slightly smaller and came in a range of shaded pastel colours. Responding to Implantech's glitzy announcement alert, Connor scheduled the in-person appointment at his local pharma-hub. When his time came, he selected a Salmon Blush Gen 2 Capsule, precisely the colour he imagined his lower intestine to be, washed it down with a glass of chilled almond milk, and headed home to await the calibrating diagnostic results.

It identified him as borderline Type 2 diabetic and had detected pre-cancerous cells in his colon.

"Oh, Christ!" Connor cried. "I'm going to be so rich!"

The diet and exercise programme laid out before him appeared relentless, but the Improvements score it was correlated against was everything he'd dreamed it would be, and more. He set to work right away.

Three months in, and Connor hadn't felt so good in years. Six months in and his pre-diabetic indicators were nearly normal again. The new habits he'd been forming in the programme felt so great they inspired him to improve still further. He was completing his eleventh month and feeling fitter than ever before when they announced the award. A major wave of new partners would be joining the programme and a special livestream event with a lottery for high-improvement participants would be held to celebrate. The winner would have their pick from the Supreme Rewards tier for free.

I wonder if I'm in with a chance of that, thought Connor, as a notification announcing his place on the shortlist appeared on his screen.

***

"And last, but certainly not least. He's beaten diabetes, he's beaten cancer, he's the most-improved man in the nation's north and east. Let's welcome Connor!"

"Hello there, Geraldine. How are you?"

"Not as healthy as you, Connor. How could I be?"

A mixture of remote audience laughter and clapping bursts, then clips out, from Connor's telestream console. Geraldine grins and shrugs her shoulders, feigning a half-embrace.

"Congratulations to you, Connor. Have you given any thought as to which reward you'd claim if you win tonight?"

"Ah, yes, Geraldine. I want to travel. If I won, I'd take the Orbital Escape vacation."

"What? Up there with all those unhealthy Riches, Connor?"

The laughter and clapping comes again. Geraldine looks skyward and presses her index finger against pursed lips.

"Oh, I'll be fine, Geraldine. I mean, I've had all my shots."

Bits 'n' Bacon

Stephen Oram

HIS WIFE, Helen, had died a horrible death, and yet Yoshi, his plastic puppy, refused to stop showing videos of her across its forehead.

"Bacon?" said Andy to this modern-day guard dog, which he loved and loathed in equal measure.

"No."

"Then add it to the shopping list."

"No. I have analysed the effect it could have on your health conditions, and it's a *no*."

The sound of a key in the door distracted them.

"Look who I found," called the nurse. Andy seemed to remember this one was called Jane. Or was it Jenny? Whoever she was, she wasn't the doctor he craved. He hadn't looked one of those in the eyes for years. Ellie stood behind her, making those tiny gesticulations that the local gangs seemed to think passed for a greeting. Andy beckoned his granddaughter and the nurse to come in.

"This bloody fake dog won't order me any bacon," he said, as they took off their coats and settled in. He stared at Yoshi. Did he really need a robot to optimise his life, not to mention to act as the God-given gatekeeper to his fridge? Mind you, he'd seen how Helen had painfully deteriorated without access to this level of care, and he'd certainly do anything to avoid that creeping onslaught of disintegration.

"We've updated our terms and conditions," said the nurse. "We need your permission to continue using Yoshi's data."

"What's changed?"

"Does it matter?" said Ellie.

"Mr—" The nurse glanced at the strip of tech pinned to her blouse. "—Mr Takkor. The data pays for Yoshi and all the care it gives you. Not a bad deal, if you ask me."

"Yes. Yes, I know. Go ahead. Upload at your convenience."

She nodded, and after glancing at the chip on his wrist, which displayed his current aggregated state of health, she added, "Good to see you're green today." She tilted her head towards Ellie. "She's green too." Andy frowned, reminded that Helen had found it impossible to come off red.

The nurse checked that Yoshi and the fridge were both up-to-date and once she was satisfied that everything was in order, she left Andy and Ellie to it.

"Well," said Andy, as he felt his wrist chip taking its daily blood sample. "What shall we do today?"

Ellie was a good lass really, even if she did run a bit wild at times, so when she suggested they go somewhere that she was sure her granddad would appreciate, Andy agreed.

They set off on their walk, chatting away while improving his health score.

"Here we are," said Ellie as they reached the entrance to an alleyway.

"Where?"

"One of ours. You'll see."

Ellie led the way, stepping around the neat piles of recyclable food packaging which, when scanned, would predict how the contents might affect your health. Each pre-packaged piece of food would have contained nanotech that registered its passage through the human, providing the health company with certainty on who was eating what. Stacked as they were, they looked inconsequential, but were an essential element of the health system, and their aggregated data was the reason Andy wasn't allowed to buy his bacon.

A door with a red light came into view. "A brothel?"

"Of sorts," said Ellie, "but a surprising one."

Inside, the tall, elegant woman who was running the show led them past rooms packed full of people. Andy paused outside one of them, where a young woman scanned a packet of crisps and passed the contents to the man opposite her. He grabbed a handful, crammed them in his mouth, and, leaving it wide open, he chewed loudly. He shoved the bowl in front of him to one side, paid her a little extra, and spat the masticated mess onto the dirty floor. She gathered it up, grimaced, and swallowed it in one gulp.

"My consumption workers take the hit," said their host. "After my clients have had the pleasure inside their mouths. Interested?"

"This way," said Ellie, guiding Andy away by the elbow.

In the next room, a sumptuous spread of sizzling bacon and buttered bread was laid out on a long table. Empty packets were piled at one end, where a group of sickly individuals hung around with hopeful glints in their eyes and red chips on their wrists.

"Your treat," said Ellie.

"I don't understand," said Andy.

Their host smiled. "A bacon sandwich. Absolute top-end. No tracking tech. Expensive."

"Home-grown? Black market?"

Ellie coughed. "You must be kidding. They give you ten years for that and only two for robbing the rich. These are from the super-rich homes in Mayfair. You know they avoid having to swallow tech by paying a sort of insurance premium on their food? It's a service the companies offer to certain postcodes. You purchase for your family and can then fool the system by allocating the packaging to whoever you want. All the family gets free healthcare, so long as they're green."

Andy gazed at the luxurious spread.

The woman gently pushed him forward. "You pay us and you eat, but we pretend our workers ate it. Everyone wins."

"They look ill."

She laughed. "Comes with the job. They're excluded from health care because of their diet."

Andy turned to Ellie. "I can't afford this," he said.

"You can. Sell them a snapshot of your health data and you can afford two or three."

"I already sold it to the nurse."

"Data can be sold more than once, you know."

"But it'll be flawed if it doesn't include everything I've eaten."

"You think they care?" said Ellie. "C'mon, a cheeky bacon sandwich never hurt anyone. Just sell the data and enjoy the bacon."

Andy leant across to the wrappers to see exactly what his data would buy, and his chip turned red.

The woman pulled his arm back. "You clumsy fool, you've scanned the package. You're matched to it now and you'll have to take the hit."

"Granddad!"

"It was your idea," said Andy, staring at his wrist. "And a bloody stupid one, too."

Meals on Wheels

Britta Schulte

"HELLO?"

...

"Oh, hi, Ben, so good to hear from you! How is that husband of yours doing?"

...

"Really? That is great, he deserved that."

...

"Yeah, we are doing OK here as well, thanks for asking."

...

"Sure, I have time to chat. You might want to grab a drink, though; I have already opened a bottle."

...

"No, no, nothing bad, just my mother is driving me bonkers again. You know the story."

...

"Haven't I told you yet that she has to wear one of these smart bracelets now? ... What? ... Yes, since she had that fall."

...

"God, have we not spoken for so long? OK, let me start at the beginning. Mother had a fall a couple of months ago. Not too bad, but she had to have a little operation on her hip. It

33

was a rather small thing. She just stayed at the hospital overnight and then she was done with it. You know Claire, she normally is the centre of attention everywhere she goes, dancing, chatting, helping others. But in hospital, she was really quiet. Not herself at all. Her doctor got really worried how this might affect her in the long run. So, he prescribed her one of those smart bracelets. The ones that measure…well, everything, really. The armband measures her heart rate and stuff and there are a couple of sensors in the house that connect to the bracelet. Anything out of the ordinary will trigger a notification. If there is a problem or just something changes in her behaviour, the emergency contact will be alerted. And, well, I am my mother's emergency contact. I wasn't too sure how I felt about that, but there wasn't really anyone else. You know I love her to bits, but we have had so many fights and quarrels in the past. We have a bit of a problem setting our boundaries. I was afraid that this might make it worse. And yeah, sometimes it does."

…

"No, it is not at all like those emergency buttons. Can you imagine Claire wearing one of those ugly things around her neck? No, no, it is actually quite stylish. You can change the colour of the wristband and she is absolutely into colour matching, so she has four or five now."

…

"What? Yes of course she picked the house sensors too, haha. And the idea is that you do not have to push a button, but that it actually detects emergencies on its own. Maybe even notifies you before it comes to that. It sounds like such a good idea, but whoever designed it has clearly never met my mother."

…

"What she does? Nothing. Nothing out of the ordinary. But for her standards, not mine. I get a couple of notifications every day as the system tries out to figure her out. I told you she has a problem with her hips, right? But she discovered Tinder a while ago, and now she uses it like other people use meals on wheels. She cannot go out much, but she gets a lot of visitors and, well, not all come for tea and biscuits, so I get a lot of notifications that she is in and out of bed at unusual times. Imagine, I get a notification that says: Your mother just laid down outside her usual sleeping times, maybe you want to check on her? So, for the first few times, I tried to get in touch with her, which normally meant that she got quite angry with me or tried to ignore me. Which I get now, I mean you are just getting in the mood and then the fucking phone rings. Nobody likes that. But when she called back, she would tell me all about her newest conquest, so now I know. Too much. John and me have started to call the ringtone of the application the Get Lucky, because I can tell you quite often when my mother is going to…I mean, don't get me wrong, I am really happy for her, that she is living her life to the fullest, but maybe I do not need to know all that."

…

"Yeah, I know. But there are some other things I just don't like. I mean, it wants to prevent illnesses and someone being in trouble. But I also get a couple of notifications that apparently she is day-drinking and asking whether I want to check on her. And honestly, I assume she is just having a good time with someone who brought a bottle over and even if not …she is a grown-up. I mean, what am I to do with the information? I hope she would tell me if she was feeling down…and if not, that is kind of her business too, right? But yeah, so I get a lot of notifications that I cannot really switch off in case something really bad happens. She cannot switch it off because it is linked to her health insurance now and she loses benefits when she switches it off. Her premiums have gone down because the device interprets a lot of her activity as exercise."

...

"I know, it is quite cool, that she has always been so open about her sexuality and all. So, it is not like this is news to me, it is just the level of information that I get from these sensors is quite stunning. And today, it just went over the top. Today, we found a new feature of the device. When the mics detect something they cannot interpret, they send a snippet to you. For you to decide if you want to intervene. AI is not there all the way, is it? So, today I had the pleasure to listen to a guy spanking my mother. Or my mother spanking a guy. They were both equally excited, so it was hard to tell from the sound alone. And you know what, I get it. I get what the thing wants to do. But how is it to know what I might want to know and what is really none of my business?"

...

"Yeah, that is quite tough, isn't it? But anyways, maybe enough of my mother's sex life? I assume you know more now than you wanted. What is new with you?"

Afterword

Angus Fraser

"I NEVER think of the future. It comes soon enough," Albert Einstein said. He was clearly a genius but for me, as an inventor and app developer, just going with the flow and accepting the deep tech that is thrown at us daily is simply not an option.

Clearly the problem is that "The future is not what it used to be," as the author Robert Graves remarked, referring to the evaporation of our early, somewhat overoptimistic expectations of the inherent goodness of technological progress. Every step forward in health tech, like the ability to use implants for monitoring sugar by diabetics, is offset by risks, for example that DNA test results could cause our insurance premiums to soar. The future of health tech is sneaky; it lures us in with the rose-colored promises of new tech only to spin out the story in a completely unpredictable direction.

However, any observer of the relentless data-snooping march of social media and health apps would have noticed the ever-tightening noose of surveillance on our lives, particularly in the medical area. It was hiding in full light, out in the open, but the rollout of those data capturing techniques was so gradual that we as a society have missed the tipping point.

Data and code can be oppressive weapons, with health apps tempting us in only to grab the data and turn the apparently helpful tool into a nanny-state hook into our lives. In the story "Bits 'n' Bacon", by Stephen Oram, we see the tension between a healthy lifestyle – following a healthy diet means being a good, cost-effective citizen, not burdening the state health service with health problems - and the freedom to eat what you want.

But it is not just the state that has designs on our personal freedom, sacrificing it on the altar of the collective good.

Back in 2000, Bill Joy, then chief computer scientist at Sun Microsystems, noted in *Wired* magazine: "The twenty-first century technologies - genetics, nanotechnology, and robotics (GNR) - are so powerful that they can spawn whole new classes of accidents and abuses. Most dangerously, for the first time, these accidents and abuses are widely within the reach of individuals and small groups. They will not require large facilities or rare raw materials. Knowledge alone will enable the use of them."

"Virtually Dead", by Jules Owen, reflects an unlikely but no longer implausible situation in which the lack of integration of health and ID (identity systems) leads to a living, healthy person being "cancelled" without recourse.

Another example of unintended consequences is the use of online health reward units as currency or as a stake to win holidays or a discount on health service. In the chilling story "Health Miles", by Benjamin Greenaway, we see how someone can be tempted to install an invasive implant monitoring their health data in exchange for a very minor gain such as a discount on public transport or credits on a Netflix stream.

In countries where health service is free it is easy to see tensions between individuals' free will and choices that harm the collective good. I am not looking forward to a referendum on those options.

The tensions of health care costs, elderly care costs, and rising numbers of people who need that care as our populations age are explored in "Meals on Wheels", by Britta Schulte. Automated care is delivered based on audio-visual surveillance of a grandmother, whose privacy, right to her own life, and right to autonomy are constrained because the family is only able to afford automated surveillance and alert tools, not a carer. The dignity of privacy becomes a thing of the past, sacrificed on the altar of efficiency and cost-saving for both the local community health care system and family members' wallets.

The tools that exist to date, with few exceptions, detect a condition or situation. The next stage, as exemplified by blood sugar monitors now on the market, is suggestion. With this type of device, a remedial course of action is suggested when it detects a particular set of circumstances. The final decision to act is left up to the person interpreting the data. The final stage in this progression would be to intercede directly with treatment. In the case of a blood sugar monitor, this would mean a system that maintains the correct blood sugar level based on the person's observed state, an entirely real-time, closed loop system to maintain health.

I believe the adoption of such technology should remain local, by which I mean that the closed loop system should be under the control of the user. The data that is gathered and used should remain inside the closed loop unless the user "actively" decides to share it. A blood sugar monitor's efficiency might be improved if measurement and treatment data were shared to improve the treatment's AI model. However, the user who provides the information should be able to expect that the data's usage is strictly limited. The data they provide is not a commodity that can be further sold and traded.

I have developed devices using facial recognition to monitor for use of masks during covid, so I am fully aware of the dangers when data gathering is driven by health concerns. But I deeply hope that in both my technological invention practice and in bigger health settings we will always prioritise privacy and agency over costs – after all, these new technologies have a huge potential to help, as long as they don't make us somewhat less human by depriving us of our right to stay private or our right to free will.

The assumption of privacy needs to be the mantra of this emerging industry. Personally, rather than Einstein, I choose to side with Alan Kay, the inventor of tablet technology, who said, "The best way to predict the future is to build it." By actively participating, we get at least a fighting chance to create the future that we actually want to live in.

PART 2:
Recovery of
the High Street

Viral Advertising

George Jacobs

THE CITYCONNECT train breathed to a stop at Central Station. All the passengers got off, Ren included. This was the innermost stop – the train would now head back the way it had come till it reached the outermost suburbs, then repeat, programmed to execute the journey endlessly. It was but one spoke on the CityConnect wheel.

Ren made his way through the crowd to the e-bus stop marked for city section A. There was only so far the trains could penetrate the urban sprawl, what with planning permission how it was, making roads a necessity. The driverless bus pulled up, and Ren boarded along with about twenty others. He was dressed casually, doing his best to be just another face in the crowd, nothing anyone would remember.

His phone buzzed as it linked with the e-bus, but Ren found a seat before he took it out of his pocket. He only had a few seconds left to choose whether to play a game of Fruit Crusher, or have the £2 e-bus ride fee deducted from his account before the latter option was chosen by default. He pressed to accept the game.

It took only thirty seconds for Ren to fail the game's first level. "Do you wish to continue?" asked the app. "Only £1 for three continues." No, Ren didn't want to continue. Yes, he was sure.

His terrible score was then displayed in comparison to everyone who'd played on the e-bus that day. Judging by the scores of the top five, some people had spent a lot more than £1 on continues. Ren closed the app and dimmed the brightness – it was vital his phone didn't heat up enough to damage the payload.

People got on, people got off. Most people were on their phones, the bus pretty silent. But the e-bus chat was buzzing away with comments, and Ren quickly muted it. He rode the e-bus all the way into the city centre, to the high street. That's where his target was.

The centre was busy, always was. Cafes, salons, games rooms, pickup points, amongst much else. A hubbub of conversation, laughter, and music filled the air, punctuated by the occasional cheer as someone won a match in the arcade. All the businesses were local, though you'd not know that from the signs. Local Authority regulations meant everything within the city centre limits had to be independent and locally owned. It didn't say anything about what those local businesses could advertise, however.

Ren walked past hairdressers whose windows were covered with interactive adverts for fast-food chains, and newsstands emblazoned with QR codes promoting out-of-town car dealerships. His phone buzzed from notifications from the centre wifi, promising discounts, loyalty schemes, and links to online catalogues. Beneath Ren's feet, vast warehouses thrummed with activity, robots moving items from storage to lifts which transported them up to the privately owned pickup points as and when they were ordered.

The north end of the high street was dominated by Dotty's Coffee Shop. Dotty had a popular online presence, marketing herself as everyone's lovable grandma. That online presence was something she'd been able to leverage into the best corporate sponsorships, which in turn made her the queen of the city centre. Most local businesses had no hope; they couldn't afford the city rents without risk-averse, big business support.

Heading past the wraparound tablet and phone adverts that danced across the interior screens, Ren found a table at Dotty's and ordered a latte through the app. Around him, people sipped their coffees, a good many of them playing with electronic gadgets. One corner of the shop was given over to VR, where a large group of teenagers were playing the latest game. Ren felt a mixture of pity and loathing for them.

From the Dotty's app, Ren opened up the master catalogue. Dotty's offered the opportunity to trial electronic goods from several international chains. If patrons liked them they could order them directly through the app, getting a referral discount, and collect them from the pickup point just outside.

"Your coffee, sir." A young waitress placed the drink on the table.

"Thanks," said Ren.

"Would you like to sample any products from our sponsors today? We have the new Nova S3 today, exclusive to Dotty's."

"Actually, yes. I would like to test that phone, please."

"No problem, sir. I'll have someone bring one to your table."

Ren didn't have long to wait. Dotty's was a slick operation, despite the old lady branding. The phone was a nice bit of kit, very powerful, very stylish, very expensive. There was no danger of theft, though; anything removed from the shop would brick itself and summon the police.

As subtly as he could, Ren removed the memory wafer from his phone, and transferred it to the Nova S3, popping the slot cap and closing it up with a practised motion of his hands, his baggy hoodie shielding the operation from Dotty's cameras.

Next it was time to drain the battery. Ren activated everything he could think of that was heavy on the power, continuing to tap away at the phone, ordering another coffee, then a croissant. At last, the phone flashed a warning that it needed charging. Ren got up, handed the phone to one of the waiters, then went to catch his e-bus.

He was on the CityConnect by the time he received a push notification from the local news site. Dotty's had been hacked. For over half an hour, patrons had been redirected from the master catalogue. The tweaks to the search algorithms had been subtle, taking time to notice, funnelling customers away from the big business and towards the online portals of local businesses. Before Dotty's staff realised what had occurred, hundreds of items had been ordered from independent sellers for home delivery, rather than bought from Dotty's sponsors for pickup.

The news had reached out to some of the beneficiaries, but so far no one had claimed responsibility. Business owners were professing ignorance of the entire thing, though Dotty's corporate backers had promised to get to the bottom of things.

Ren smiled. By now the memory wafer would have disintegrated from the little heat generated by charging the phone. But its work had been done, uploading Ren's program to Dotty's cloud. They wouldn't get to the bottom of it. Ren was just a good Samaritan doing what he could. This wasn't the first thing, wouldn't be the last. He wouldn't let the high street kill the true independents.

Togetherness

Mark Huntley-James

I REMEMBER when deliveries used to come to my flat – the waiting in, watching the live tracking info, trying to guess how much the driver put his toe down on the A30. Watching my new shoes overtake my groceries at the Devon-Cornwall border, and making bets on the race with Wrinkles, my hamster. All he ever did was eat and run on the wheel, so how did he know my shoes would detour through Bodmin?

It doesn't matter. Wrinkles has gone to the great treadmill in the sky, and I've switched to GetItTogether.net. I don't bother to watch the live status updates converging on my virtual address at their consolidation depot. What's the point? The thrill of the race just isn't there.

I drove into town – it's only about fifteen minutes – and parked outside Handy's Corner Shop, next to Herd's Meat and Deli, and opposite the Virtual Pint, the last surviving businesses in town. Honestly, the only reason the pub is still in going is that they deliver, but Herd's is still going strong, because out in the sticks we still appreciate knowing which farm our burgers come from, and Mrs Handy is the hub for all the delivery consolidators. I think maybe she still sells the occasional bottle of milk.

"Hi, Mrs Handy... smartbuyer-one-three-eight-two... picking up my stuff."

Apparently a lot of users pick *smartbuyer* for a user name.

"It's Mrs Crosby, love."

"Right." I always forget that. "Sorry. My stuff?"

"Don't think I've got nothing for you, love." Mrs Handy checked all her screens, the one on her till, the one above the till, the tablet on the counter – but she is not tech-savvy, so I got my phone out in anticipation of "What's the order number?"

I showed her my details, she scanned the code, and,

"Sorry, love, that's a GetItTogether job. I'm only handling AllTogether.now, LumpItAndLikeIt.co.uk, and Virtually.Us."

"But..." I pointed to her window, with the GetItTogether logo. "I got my shopping here last week."

"I know, love. Sorry. It's just that GetItTogether cut my handling fee by half, so I just can't afford it. It's rural living, you see? City deliveries are cheap, but out here it's different."

"So where's my shopping?" According to the Together app on my phone, it was at Handy's Corner Shop. "It should be here."

Mrs Handy beckoned, held out her hand for my phone, and then stabbed at the screen. I'm not sure she really knows what she's doing.

"See, love?"

I looked, but I didn't see. "It says..."

"Here, love." She pointed precisely. "Virtual holding depot, see? GetItTogether set up a virtual address for me shop, so that's where *your* shopping is. They got it at the GetItTogether depot, pretending to be here, see?"

Yes, I did see. "So how do I get it *actually* here, instead of *virtually* here?"

"That's easy, love." Mrs Handy tapped her own tablet and then turned it round for me to see. "That's me, at GetItTogether, and that's me at AllTogether.now. So, if you've got an AllTogether account, I can just move it from there to here. Easy."

"I don't have an AllTogether account."

"What about LumpItAndLikeIt?"

I shook my head.

"Virtually.Us?"

"Nope."

"Sorry, love... do you have *any* other delivery consolidation accounts?"

"I used PackAnimal like ages ago. Absolutely ages ago. Like at least six months."

"There you go, love. Perfect." She stabbed at her tablet again. "This is my virtual AllTogether address on PackAnimal, so I can move your order across to here... then here... then *here*!"

"Fantastic. When can I pick it up?"

Mrs Handy consulted her tablet. "Well, GetItTogether will ship it out to PackAnimal tonight... so that's... Norfolk to Galway... two days tops... then PackAnimal will send it to AllTogether in Powys, so two days... then Powys will send it to their Plymouth hub... it'll be here, end of next week, no trouble. Here... I can install the HandyTracker app for you."

"Thanks, Mrs Handy."

She sighed and did things to my phone. "Love, I told you, I'm Mrs Crosby. I just bought the shop."

"Sorry. I forgot. But thanks. See you next week."

***

The HandyTracker really was fantastic. I watched my shopping go to Galway, to Powys, to Plymouth, back to Powys, Plymouth again, and finally head into Cornwall. I also opened an AllTogether account, because clearly GetItTogether has fallen apart.

That may have been a mistake.

HandyTracker synched with AllTogether, and both showed my shopping arriving at the distribution hub in Bodmin. According to HandyTracker, it then headed towards Wadebridge, putting it on track to arrive at Handy's Corner Shop, but according to AllTogether, it went down the A30 to Truro.

I texted Mrs Handy. *My shopping has got lost.*

Don't worry love, she answered an hour later. *It's just that AllTogether halved the commission. Everyone cancelled their contracts. All sorted now. See you tomorrow.*

I didn't sleep much. I had visions of my shopping in virtual orbit somewhere in the middle of Cornwall. Just after six in the morning, AllTogether pinged – your delivery is now in our Penzance depot, awaiting delivery. I refreshed the status a few times, but it was definitely right, and then HandyTracker pinged – your delivery is now ready for collection at the Handy Corner Shop.

I couldn't face breakfast and drove in to town at half eight. The Virtual Pint was busy, loading up deliveries for the day, Mr Herd was already serving his first customers, and the Handy Corner Shop still had the GetItTogether logo in the window.

"Mrs Handy!"

"Crosby, love. Mrs Crosby."

"Is it here?"

"Yes. Arrived this morning, love. See, all sorted. And I even got back with GetItTogether on a decent commission."

"Thanks, Mrs Handy."

"I think they reboxed it at Powys, but it all looks fine." She pursed her lips. "Apart from the dairy products."

"Thank you, thank you, thank you." I kissed my phone, which deleted a couple of emails and updated the AllTogether app – *your delivery is ready for collection.*

"So, love, that will be sixty-two pounds thirty for the transfer." Mrs Handy pursed her lips again. "Did you want a couple of bottles of milk?"

The Little Shop That Could

Vaughan Stanger

MILENA STARED at the flashing sign hovering above the exhibition's entrance, then glanced over her shoulder.

"Mum, why is it called moths?"

"M-O-T-H-S stands for the Museum of the High Street. I did say that's where we're going."

"What's a high street?"

"You've heard of Amazon?"

Milena nodded.

"Well, a high street was like a mini-Amazon arranged on either side of a road."

The double doors swept open to reveal a long, gritty-floored hallway, with lots of signs and doors and tall windows. Fluffy holo-clouds floated beneath the pale blue ceiling.

"So, are those shops?"

Her mum chuckled. "That's right. Your gran worked in one selling cosmetics and medicines."

Milena's gran joined them, having successfully exchanged crypto for something called "hard cash" outside. She pointed towards a blue sign with curvy white lettering.

"Boots was the last shop to close where I lived." She sounded sad.

A weird-looking robot made of metal rods wobbled up to them. One of its wheels was spinning like an app that had crashed. Its cyber-eyes blinked a greeting.

"Can I help you?"

Its cheerful voice made Milena smile.

"No, thanks," said her mum. "We don't need a guide."

"It's not too late to change your—"

"No thanks!"

The robot wobbled away, searching for other visitors. Milena had counted five so far – all adults.

"What was that thing?"

"A shopping trolley," said her mum. "We won't need it."

"Too pushy," her gran said.

Milena's mum groaned. "How about we do some window shopping?"

Whatever that was.

"Okay."

After they'd walked past several shopfronts, Milena pointed to one topped by a bright green sign.

"What did Oxfam sell?"

Her gran sighed. "Second-hand clothes and books, mostly."

"What's second-hand?"

"Stuff people donated because they didn't need it anymore."

Milena wrinkled her nose. "Who would buy that?"

"Other people."

Her frown deepened. "But why?"

The two adults exchanged glances.

Her mum said, "Oxfam helped poor people."

"Oh, I see."

At least Milena thought she did. She knew poor people were extinct. A bit like moths and tigers and *both* Amazons.

"Can we go in?"

"I'm not sure—"

"Nonsense," said Milena's gran. "We're here to shop!"

Milena followed her inside. Ignoring the rails of holo-clothes, she headed straight for the tall shelves at the back.

Eyes wide, she said, "Are those *real* books?"

Her gran shook her head. "I shouldn't think so."

Milena reached up for one with a statue of a tiger on its cover.

Her mum snapped, "Don't touch!"

The book disappeared. Her gran laughed.

"Too late!"

Milena's mum sighed. "I *knew* that would happen."

Outside the shop, the wonky-wheeled trolley waited for them, its cyber-eyes still blinking. The holo-book floated within its metal frame.

"Please pay for your shopping after you leave this exhibition."

Both adults chuckled.

Her gran said, "Exit via…"

"…gift shop!"

Milena didn't understand what was so funny, but it didn't matter. She had been shopping. That's what counted.

***

The gift shop contained lots of shelves and clothes rails, all empty. An Ubi hummed in the corner. Milena frowned because their trolley was now empty.

"Where's my book?"

Her gran smiled. "We have to pay for it first."

"You know, I could still grab the code so we could ubi it at home," her mum said. "That wouldn't cost anything."

Milena crossed her arms. "But it wouldn't be shopping!"

Her gran nodded vigorously. "Milena's right! Don't worry, dear, I'll pay."

"Are you sure?"

"It would be my pleasure."

Milena's mum sighed. "Okay, just this once."

When her gran fed a plastic note into the indicated slot, the Ubi purred like Milena's virtual cat.

Her mum frowned as though she now regretted the visit.

"No wonder this place is closing next month. No one *really* misses shopping."

"I do," said her gran.

"Ha! You just miss eating out."

"Well yes, that too!"

Milena frowned. "What's eating *out*?"

Her gran replied, "After the shops disappeared, people still went to the high street to eat. But the Great Pandemic of '31 ended that. Soon afterwards, the government gave every household an Ubi, so there wasn't any reason to eat out anymore."

"But your gran loves a touch of nostalgia," Milena's mum said. "She thought you might enjoy this exhibition."

Her gran gave Milena a serious look. "You did enjoy it, didn't you?"

Milena nodded but her attention was now on the delivery tray. The Ubi had stopped purring. Her book slid out. She snatched it up before *it* disappeared too.

Every page delivered magic. She gazed in wonder at the statues of lions and elephants and other extinct things.

Her mum tapped the book's cover. "Our Ubi could make any of those."

Milena shook her head. "I've got a *much* better idea!"

She didn't want something made for her. She wanted to make something for *herself*. For that, she'd need some modelling clay.

Their Ubi could provide it but only if she recycled other stuff first. Unless her gran topped up her feedstock allowance. And once she'd made her animals, she would need somewhere to display them.

Happily, she had an idea about that.

***

The elderly man accompanying the boy frowned.

"Are you *sure* you want it?"

The boy nodded.

"Why?"

"'Cos it wasn't made by an Ubi. Jamie's got two already!"

The man muttered something about a "fad."

"Please!"

The boy didn't seem to mind that the unicorn wasn't one of Milena's better efforts. Keeping up with demand was difficult. The supply of clay was no longer a problem, now that the Ubi which owned the MOTHS building had approved her business plan, but she could only skip so much school.

The man turned to Milena. "Is this thing *really* an Ubinot?"

She smiled at him. "Yes, it is."

He sighed while placing his money on the counter. Milena wrapped the unicorn in paper and handed it to the boy.

Once they'd gone, she waved at her gran, who was standing on the opposite side of the "road" but too busy to respond while welcoming families into the café.

The high street was booming again.

***

During their journey home, Milena asked her gran about fads.

Within a week, she'd opened a new shop selling second-hand Ubinots.

The Time Travelling Milkman

Jane Norris

THE OPENING question my boss asked me was "What is the first material you meet in life? something essential to our survival … the only substance we both produce and consume?" I knew he was talking about milk, but I hadn't quite thought of it that way. He was right though, it's odd stuff, milk. It often reveals how we treat the world around us. It shows how people's attitudes to food change their high streets. Milk, our most intimate material, is one we have a strange relationship with.

Before I started in this business, milk was a living being. Back before the industrial revolution, I didn't have a job. People only drank human milk. That milk was a vital bridge to physical independence and survival. It contained the wisdom of my family bacterial resistance, offered nourishment for my bones, lactose sugars to grow my brain. The live and volatile "being" that was cow's milk, was only given occasionally to the sick. Dairies had traditionally sold cheese, not milk.

My first job was in 1810 in London. I sold a new luxury material, cow's milk. I worked in a small cowshed with five cows. My customers knew my name and the cows' names, and which cows from the sheds along The Strand in London gave the best-quality milk. Those were good times. On saints' days when I had some time off, I would walk across the fields to St. Martin's church to chat to a girl I knew. Everyone in those days knew that milk's flavour changed with the seasons. People understood milk as alive with its own characteristics and demands. Back then, your milk would have gone "off" in a day.

But fifty years later in the mid-nineteenth century when eighty percent of milk was produced in towns, attitudes to milk had changed. I was kicked out of my job. The rows of cowsheds from St Martin-in-the-Fields to the Strand were cleared, to make London supposedly more hygienic. People said milk was now unhealthy and dangerous. It was blamed for the epidemics of typhoid, scarlet fever and tuberculosis sweeping Europe. I remember the spring of 1862, when I heard from a mate in a coffee shop that Louis Pasteur had learned to heat milk to high temperatures for short periods, killing the dangerous microbes. This was good news as it would keep me in some employment. But the heat that killed the bad microbes killed all the good microbes too – in fact, it killed the milk. I was sad to see our relationship with milk change. It was no longer seen as a living being with microbacteria to aid digestion and stimulate the immune system. Once it was dead, it was sold in sterilised glass bottles. It certainly lasted longer, but it was now just a product to make money. I got a job working for one of the big dairies out of town that collected milk from the farmers, treated it, and delivered it in. I just had to put the right number of bottles on the right doorstep.

This was a stable job for many decades. The only thing that changed was that I swapped my horse and cart for an electric milk float and used to whirr up and down the increasingly busy streets of London. I got up early to try and miss the rush-hour traffic, as people travelled to and from the big offices and shops they worked in. But things change, people's attitudes to milk have shifted once more. Milk production became so industrialised that I didn't make enough money on my personalised rounds. So I lost that job and now work at the Sainsburys Local stacking big plastic cartons of milk into the cooling cabinets. Some people still buy big two-litre containers, but the numbers are reducing. They have found that drinking this dead white liquid has led to lactose intolerances. People are starting to avoid it. I notice the shelves of almond "milk" are increasing.

I guess as a response to this, the big industrial milk companies have converted dead milk into hundreds of different commercial opportunities. Milk is now marketed as a probiotic medicine by artificially adding the microbes back in; it is fortified with vitamins – suggesting it was lacking; it has had its fat reduced - as if it had too much or the wrong sort; it has been homogenised - as if it was somehow unacceptably diverse.

But this could be different, if people respected the live and transitory nature of the living being that is milk. If people want to benefit from cow's milk, we need to keep it clean, fresh, and alive. We would then know the many benefits it brings to digestion, or to those living with eczema, asthma, calcium deficiency, lactose intolerance, perhaps even Alzheimer's, and many other chronic conditions. But this would require a different relationship with cows, it would mean caring for our milk herds, ensuring they were naturally healthy, giving cows fresh clean grass and hay to eat, not processed grain pellets full of antibiotics. This would then oblige us to stop factory farming. This would then change our use of town centres. Small milk herds would have to move closer to the consumer again, as the milk would have a shorter shelf life once more. We would need small fields with a handful of cows and a shed selling fresh milk, where local high streets now have empty shuttered Poundland stores. People might come again to know mine and my cows' names and be able to tell the difference in taste between their creamy summer and thinner winter milk.

In a post-pandemic world, as many people continue to work and shop from home, local high streets need to produce healthier food more locally. "Live milk" could in turn enliven our high streets. We might start to respect milk again, understand it as seasonal, with its own rights. And I might get my happiest job back, working on The Strand with my five cows.

Low-Down on the High Street

David Gullen

ARTHUR STOOD on the doorstep and watched another delivery drone attempt to deliver his order. Out of nowhere a pirate drone dropped through the clouds, capture-net extended beneath it like a dragonfly's legs. The delivery drone released a cluster of single-use biodegradable countermeasures, but a second pirate drone swept them from the sky. Moments later the delivery drone was snagged in the net. Rotors tangled, it hung helplessly as the pirate drone rose into the clouds and disappeared.

Angry and frustrated, Arthur called Kamal – again.

"Look, I know it's not your fault, I just want my order... No, I don't want a refund, it's a gift, my granddaughter's birthday... Try again? I suppose, but when? Her birthday's next week.

"Isn't there anywhere I can pick it up?

"All right, I understand. Maybe next time."

***

"That's a typical scenario." Kamal paused playback and sat down next to Rosamunde, his wife. "And it's getting worse. Five percent losses last year, eight percent so far this year and fourteen projected for next quarter. Yes, drones are cheap. Yes, we can factor in losses, and yes, our drone suppliers are designing new models with better defence capabilities, but we can't keep–"

"Who's responsible?"

"Kids for kicks, youth gangs, and now, organised crime."

"Kids?"

"Drones are cheap."

"What are the police doing?"

"What police?" Kamal leaned heavily on the table. "Roz, I'm not sure we can keep going. It won't be long before one in ten of everything we make is stolen in transit, then one in eight."

It had long been their dream to run their own leather crafts business – bags, notebooks, and cases. Four years ago they'd taken the plunge. Neither of them wanted to work for some big corporation again.

Roz gave a heartfelt sigh. "And I suppose if we put up our prices we'll price ourselves out of the market."

***

That weekend Kamal and Roz visited Kamal's parents.

"It's not looking good, Mum," Kamal said when Lucy, the younger of his mothers, asked how things were going.

"What are your choices?"

"There's only one – buy into the big business drone convoys. That's twenty percent of your turnover gone straight away," Roz said. "And besides, we always wanted to–"

"Go it alone." Kamal's mothers held each other's hands and smiled into each other's eyes. "We know exactly what you mean."

It was a good evening despite their worries. With Lucy and Mehnoor it was easy to forget they were Kamal's parents and see them as good older friends.

"You know, my father used to work as a delivery driver back when the shops were still in the street," Mehnoor said.

"That would work," Kamal said thoughtfully. "But it would take all day and one of us wouldn't be making."

***

All next week Roz and Kamal worked hard. Orders came in, delivery drones went out, and most of them arrived. Most, but not all. Every small business was in the same situation, forums were full of worried people. Roz watched the "Arthur" scenario again and again. Something kept pulling her back to it, a feeling there was something she had missed.

She woke up at 5am. Unable to sleep, she slipped out of bed and gathered her clothes so as not to wake Kamal. Half an hour later he came into the kitchen.

"Everything all right? I woke up and you weren't there."

"Yes, great." She took a breath. "I think I know what we need to do."

Kamal made more tea. "Tell me."

"Arthur said he'd collect if he could."

Kamal held up his hand. "I don't want people coming to our home."

"Me neither. I think we should set up a stall in the old high street, tell everyone we're going to be there, emails, texts, app posts, and they can come collect their orders. Also, we can offer a discount, we should at first, anyway, just to get things going, but it should cost less to do this than run drones and keep replacing them, and—" Roz smiled and sat back. "I'm babbling, aren't I?"

"No." Kamal grinned. "Well, yes. It's a great idea but will people come out just for us?"

"I don't mean just us, I mean everyone in the same situation." She went to the window, too excited to sit. "All the local makers. Once a week, maybe twice, a pop-up high street."

"It will take some organisation—"

Roz held up her phone. "I've already started."

Two weeks later the old high street held a presence from twenty different makers. Some just to test the water, others hoping to sell hot food and drinks, and most, like Roz and Kamal, to hand over the goods they'd made and already been paid for.

A bare scatter of people turned up in the first hour, wanderers, the curious. Nobody came to Kamal and Roz's stall. Roz walked between the other makers' pitches with feelings of impending doom. This had been her idea, she had persuaded most of the people here today to come. Nobody seemed too despondent. Yet.

Then more people started to arrive. Ones and twos, then tens and twenties. By mid-morning a crowd moved among the stalls. Roz and Kamal handed out their goods and, for the first time, met the people they had been selling to.

"Hello, Kamal."

"Arthur! How are you? The notebook–?"

"It's fine, my granddaughter loved it. There's something else I want and I wondered if you could make it for me."

This was something unanticipated, a good thing. "Let me buy you a coffee and you tell me what you want."

"Hot chocolate?"

"Sure."

Kamal took in the boarded-up shops, wind-blown litter, and weed-infested planters. A burst of optimism filled him. Next week he would organise a group to sweep up and replant, it was to everyone's benefit.

They ordered, found a table, and sat down.

"It's good to meet you, Arthur. What did you have in mind?"

The Crunch

Stephen Oram

JAKE'S MOUTH is full of toothpaste when his Gran calls. He quickly rinses, pops his toothbrush in its holder, and his oral health is broadcast to his fan base.

"Hey," she says. "Good luck. Not that you'll need it."

"Thank you." He blurs the screen. "Sorry, I need to get dressed."

In the background his gran is going on about how much better things are compared to her day: she loves being able to see her doctor, dentist, and chemist all in one visit—it's old news, but he loves her and lets her ramble on—she can pop into the college or the library, the family entertainment is fantastic, and those shopper's rooms where she can order clothes and stuff from all over the place and then return what she doesn't want are amazing. He brings back the visuals and she claps. "You look wonderful," she says, "totally a town councillor in the making."

And get noticed by Gerry, he thinks. "Must dash," he says.

"Are we meeting in town for supper?"

"Yup. Full family, I heard."

"Great. Don't forget, if you lose you'll shame us all. Me and your mother and your children when they come. It's a town that remembers." She winks.

He shudders and leaves the flat as quickly as he can, confident that his best friend Mark can help boost his popularity. After all, a trend-predicting data entrepreneur with an eye for fashion might be exactly what he needs.

Out on the streets it's a lot busier than usual, but the border of the town centre seems to be coping admirably, recognising subscribers who are paid-up members and taking a fee from those who aren't.

Mark's new house is in a surprising part of town, but then he does have an uncanny knack of moving into a place just before the rent becomes fully funded through a town planner regeneration project. As Jake approaches, he gathers the one free apple his health app allocates him from a communal tree, and tears a strip of edible leaves from a vertical garden. Lunch. Mark is leaning against a lamppost, plugged in and charging. "Ready?" he asks.

"And raring," replies Jake. "Let's go."

Along the way Mark pauses at one of the recent pop-ups generated by the creative partnerships between cognitive computers, artists and entrepreneurs. Two of the town's artificial creatives are playing chess, using the shoppers as pieces on a board scattered with squares that contain surprise prizes. "Two minutes," says Mark, as he takes footage to help him turn the public datasets into a product for tourists. "So long as this smart town planner keeps flexing the business rates and placing new pop-ups to increase footfall, the data will constantly change, and I'll keep making a living," he says, followed by a big grin.

"Good for you," says Jake, tapping his foot.

"Maybe one of those prizes is a date with Gerry."

"Stop it. Come on. I need to get there."

They walk quickly to the local college where Jake waves to the crowd, inwardly worrying about being rejected and disgraced. No room for failure, as his gran would say.

The hi-tech start-ups recently housed in the local train station have fitted the candidate rooms in the college with immersive virtual reality and popularity prediction equipment. He steps into VR and chooses trousers, shirts, jackets and shoes. Each combination he tries gains a positive prediction, indicating that he should be a highly successful influencer and an advocate for their town. His gran will be pleased. The trouble is that no outfit passes the threshold for sustainability. He shifts to the second-hand clothes on offer, virtually swapping a pocket here for a pocket there and an arm here for an arm there. It's all about personalised style. None of his creations do well in the predictions until he uses the frilly collar and cuffs from a dress-shirt and attaches them to a suit jacket. It's a VR hit. He orders the clothes and thirty minutes later the jacket and shirt are delivered to the room along with the wide selection of new items he's already chosen. He sets to work on the different combinations that Mark offers until the predictions are high enough to press send, and waits to see how Gerry will react. Gerry doesn't respond.

"He hates me, I'm finished."

"You're a style guru, go with your gut," says Mark, as he gets ready to program the stitchbot to attach the collar and cuffs to the jacket. "What do you want? A place on the council or Gerry in your bed?"

"Both."

"Glutton."

"Ambitious."

As soon as the bot finishes stitching, Jake swaps the jacket he's wearing for the hybrid and faces the cameras. The predictions shoot up, but Gerry pierces Jake's elation with a stinging comment—*Boring*. His gran comments too—*Keep it popular. Remember Uncle Frank.* He doesn't, but he's heard whispered stories about the family having to disown him and delete him from the census data. He wants to please Gerry, but his gran's plea to please the crowds has hit home.

"Here, let me," he says to Mark and cuts a piece of shimmering insulation material that's growing on the walls. He hand-stitches a series of patches, making them visible and artistic. Meanwhile, the material on the wall repairs itself. The crowds love it and so does Gerry. The call comes—Jake will be incorporated into the augmented-reality parade that evening and as a newly recognised high influencer he is eligible to be voted on to the town council and to have a say in the metadata that shapes the town planner.

Gerry comments. *Fabulous to see such originality—kill all celebrity copy-catting.*

Jake laughs with delight and runs a final test to make sure nobody else has submitted a similar outfit. They haven't, so he confirms his choice with the town planner to prevent anyone copying, and relaxes.

Lounging on the sofa, he considers his apple. It is the perfect icon for his town — simple, natural, and healthy. He takes a bite. The crunch is sweet and refreshing, like life itself.

He grins. "Mate, we did it."

Afterword
Professor Rachel Armstrong

IN MORE INNOCENT times the high street was the centre of urban activity, a permanent marketplace where the skills needed to make the transactions of daily life were concentrated. Responding to broader developments in economics and culture, the various actors of rural self-sufficiency such as baker, butcher, confectioner, tailor, grocer, ironmonger, cobbler, fishmonger, and dressmaker were replaced with the local bank, post office, retail chains, franchises, department stores and supermarkets that heralded a twentieth-century global capitalist culture.

With massive population growth, the success of the urban project and corresponding increases in urban density, the intensification of consumerism through shopping centres became integral to the weekend experience of the late twentieth century but now, even these beacons of high modernist culture are under new threat. The rise of Big Tech and the availability of online shopping services have dematerialised the social and community functions associated with making a purchase, and new kinds of online communities and types of commerce have taken their place.

Today, the twenty-first century high street is fragmenting, as people retreat under the threat of pandemics or navigate the personal impacts of economic sanctions aimed at the perpetrators of World War III, whose influence is inextricably integrated into the global economy.

So where do we go from here?

Cybersalon's collection of tales from the high street of the future are rich with insights into the way we shop right now and provide fascinating, hilarious, and equally terrifying reflections on our shopping experiences yet to come.

"Viral Advertising", by George Jacobs, highlights the catastrophic tipping points in the balance of power between the global economic networks of big corporations and their suppression of true independents in the local high street, resulting in drastic action.

Such inevitable frustrations that arise from not always getting what you want, or knowing how to take something back, are explored in "Togetherness", by Mark Huntley-James, who looks at the dark spaces of delivery surveillance, where layers of tracking apps are deployed to locate lost purchases.

"The Little Shop That Could", by Vaughan Stanger, highlights the paradoxes that arise when the commercial freedoms of cyberspace intersect with the artefact of shopping centre. Exposing slippages between consumerist logic and embodied experience, different kinds of social values are revealed with the possibility of new kinds of economy.

"The Time Travelling Milkman", by Jane Norris, explores the value gap left by massively distributed and highly depersonalised shopping systems through a parallel history of a different kind of rural economy of the high street, whose entanglements of craftsmanship and care for nature are the only sustainable option to temper consumption and enable people to reconnect. Based on twenty-first century developments in science and technology, this newly-improved rurally-grounded urban economy makes possible a more nature-based way of living that is far from nostalgic but builds on the strength of its rural predecessor, proposing a healthier, kinder form of economy that ethically resituates our lives in conversation with the more than human world.

The failure of online shopping to live up to the promises is the focus for "Low-Down on the High Street" by David Gullen, who observes the frustrations of drone services in the distribution of crafts and prompting a re-evaluation of the old market stall typology as a hub for reactivating communities.

Embodying our desire for urban regeneration and new initiatives that bring back the social and political functions of the high street in an integrated way, "The Crunch", by Stephen Oram, provides a snapshot of a new kind of community that seamlessly navigates the many thresholds that exist between the virtual and the real, bringing great new energy, and offering a range of delightful cultural tropes that characterise the mixed-reality high street.

Through detailed consideration of these multiple tensions the authors consider how the online environment provides fresh insights and opportunities to establish sophisticated, new kinds of community, governance, and values, prompting us even to re-think our entire socio-political systems.

Collectively, these explorations of shopping, community, economy, politics, relationships, and our environment, offer the reader an imaginative set of tools through which to interrogate our present habits, reflect on present developments, and may help inspire the nature of the high street that is yet to come.

PART 3:
The Fabric of Community

Disconnect

Wendy M. Grossman

"WHAT ARE you doing?"

"I need a new community," I said, and then wished I hadn't.

"What, like a self-help group?"

I love my cousin Celia, really, I do, but she has no idea how little she knows. "No. It's my street..."

"Huh?"

I had just discovered that my northern cousin Celia was so lost in the sophistication of southwest London that it took me three hours to get her home from IBM Euston. She was so helpless! She had no idea how to integrate routes across neighbourhood apps, and our local cash conversions completely defeated her. Apparently Fleetwood is still using British pounds and they pay with some kind of ancient tapping ritual.

"Have her to visit," my aunt Marion had urged. "She never goes anywhere. She used to be so brilliant, but since the pandemic she just lives in that pub." So now she was here and fiddling with... was that a...*laptop*?

"You mean you're in a geoIRA?" she said.

"Uh...yes."

"Well, that's dumb."

See? Total ignorance. The Communities Rights Act, passed in 2027, strengthens communities – it's what the government said at the time, that communities proved their importance during the pandemic - and it allows us to be self-determining by bonding together in Independent Registered Associations (IRAs).

The Act creates three community types: geographical, local interest, and virtual. Geographical IRAs - geoIRAs - can opt out of council services and negotiate their own contracts for waste, recycling, and street cleaning, negotiate collectively for electricity, water, and gas, exploit "naming rights", and exercise the "right to inclusion." That one's really important, so new members share the IRA's values.

Our small cul-de-sac of twenty homes quickly voted to become a geoIRA. We then contracted with the company that owns our freeholds for what used to be council services, and the freeholder subcontracted to the council anything it couldn't make profitable. Home care, for example.

Waste pickup is more efficient, and ending the council's "townscape" classification lets the north-side houses install awnings in front so their houses are cooler in summer. The council is still a problem, though. It's prosecuting us over the awnings.

Celia interrupted: "Hey, this map says your street name is Barclays North Avenue. That's not the address you gave me."

"Oh, the council screwed us," I said.

Naming rights became a thing. My street accepted a small stipend to add "Barclays" to our Post Office street name. It only lasted a couple of months, until Barclays decided we don't generate enough data and pulled out, complaining we didn't have a CCTV camera.

Celia was at the window. "Doesn't the video billboard drive you nuts?"

"I'm hoping a new IRA will get rid of it," I said, staying focused on the screen. My personal data store didn't support any of the apps I was using, so I had to copy and paste.

IRAs began commercialising in 2031. The Southwest London Association leased our street from the freeholder and like a lot of them began requiring us to share all their data. Now, these associations are consolidating, so you don't always know where you'll end up.

I was juggling five different calculations: 1) each community's features; 2) my acceptability; 3) compatibility of values; 4) projections of each community's business model and possible future ownership; and 5) an analysis of conflicts with my five other IRAs - two local interest, three virtual.

"I'm not finding much," I said. "I think my social score is screwing me up."

"What is it?"

"In 2028, the CRA was amended to require communities to 'Know Your Members' to eliminate fraud," I said. Most IRAs outsource this to the banks and the three big credit-scoring services - Equifax, Experian, and Facebook, which bought TransUnion in 2026. "I have to submit a verified 'social score'."

"You're like Aunt Marion, still thinks I'm a barmaid. I meant, what is *your* social score?"

"Oh…um…436," I said. She looked shocked. "Look, they take off points for sleeping late, and I belong to this virtual IRA about the future of technology that they think is weird."

"And?"

"And last year I only got three out of ten on a pop quiz on my neighbours' middle names. Stop laughing!"

She looked down at her laptop and tapped a few keys.

"If you're not a barmaid, what are you?"

"I work for Commugent. The pub rents offices with terabit broadband."

My glasses crashed. "Hang on." Please, please…OK. I'd only lost the last few fields. "I just need to concentrate for a minute."

Celia was muttering something, but I tuned her out.

Suddenly she plonked her antiquated laptop on my lap. "There'll be a code in your email from 'Admin'. Type it in here."

I was glad my friends couldn't see. My screenful of accounts and calculators appeared on Celia's screen in a single view I'd never seen before. She pushed a button to project it on the ceiling. My social score now read: 700.

"Did you do that?"

"I work for Commugent. I write this shit."

"What is Commugent?"

"The fast-growing world leader in community management systems?" I still didn't get it. "This is good, actually. I never get to talk to real users." She stared at the display, and then shook her head. "Rejoin the council."

"The council is for rejects. I just - my side of the street is going TikTok. I want - not *them*."

Celia sighed. "How do people live in London? It's so far from everything and it's so pointlessly complicated… The Fleetwood council was so right."

I had read about this. Regressive northern councils called the Act a project to undermine local authorities. When it passed they put non-compete clauses in their supplier contracts. The three biggest geo-operators - TikTok, Wetherspoons, and QAnon Holdings - have referred them to the competition authorities. The case is stuck in the judicial system with our awnings.

"The Act will come for you, too," I said. "Eventually."

Friday Night Drinks at The Horse and Zoom

Peter Baran

Pól was running late from the clinic as he scanned his IDVP on his smart watch to get into the pub. This was one of the first places they used to drink in when they all worked together. It was quite different now, not least because it seemed to be half empty even on a Friday night. It retained most of its nineteenth-century charm, wood-panelled walls, and intricate glasswork. But it wasn't quite the same with the big aircon ducts, cameras, and projectors everywhere.

"Hey Pól!" Sana said. "I got you a lovely pint of Pride."

There was a pint waiting for him on their table near the back, a small serving robot toddling on the old wooden floor. Sana had picked a table by the toilets because the potential smell didn't matter to her. He popped his phone in the slot, fingerprinted in, and took a sip of his pint.

"Thanks, Sana. You know me, creature of habit," he said.

"That's an understatement," Sana said. She had a DIPA in an appropriate glass with the bottle just by it, which meant he didn't have to get into a beer bore conversation with her.

"How's your week been, Pól?" Luci said from her screen at the end of the table.

"Fine…" There was an unwritten rule that they didn't talk about work. "What are you drinking?"

"You know where you are with a margarita," Luci said.

"Under the table in about two hours," Sana said.

"It's my table," Luci said.

And her workstation, restaurant, bed, Pól thought. He couldn't remember the last time he had seen Luci in the flesh, though she was a reliable anchor for Friday night drinks.

"Is anyone else coming to the pub? Luci, you're only ten minutes away – I bet you miss the pub carpet," Pól said.

"I've explained this. It's not agoraphobia. It's claustrophilia," Luci said.

"Tony will be here in a bit," Sana said deflecting, answering his question. "Stacey's in Spain but usually remembers once she's worked out the time difference. "Not heard from Paul and Alex."

"Well it's ten a.m. in Australia, so even if they remember, it's unlikely they'll be popping in to the West End," Pól said. "I meant the *pub*-pub."

"This is the *pub*-pub," Sana said.

Pól stared at her camera, trying to get across his exasperation via body language, and part-hoping that she'd miss it to prove his point.

"Don't be like that," Sana said.

"Like what?"

"All ouchy slouchy. You're the one who likes the pub."

"We all like the pub, we've been doing Friday drinks for ten years. You booked this pub because it had all the state-of-the-art ventilation - which totally ruins the historic tin ceiling - not that you'd know because you never actually - OW."

His watch gave him a slight electrical shock and he put his pint down, unsteadily.

My camera can look up," Sana said - proving it by panning her camera up. "You're right. Ugly ductwork."

"Do we have to have this argument every week?" Luci said. "I'm getting drinks. Anyone want anything?"

"Timing!" The mini projector opposite Pól flickered on and the table ID read Dr Antony Whiteleaf briefly before it got edited to Tony.

"Same again, Luci," Pól said. His first pint had barely touched the sides. "Alright, Tony?"

"It's been a long week. And I'm on call, so just a half."

"Just the price of a normal pint, you don't have to buy this nonsense," Sana said, waving her bottle trying to get someone to ask her about her beer that contained macadamia nuts and sea spray.

"Quiet one tonight, then, Tony? I thought you might come in person," Pól said.

Tony rolled his eyes, and tried to throw a look at Sana, but his interface hadn't set his screen up spatially yet, so the thrown look went to Luci's empty screen.

"I'm on call. Anyway, I like to dress casual when I relax."

"Trousers off, Tony," Sana laughed. "I'm hosting this pub session, I can kick you out any time if you get obscene."

"Yeah, what was that shock I got about?" Pól said.

"I've updated the community rules on the pubware for my sessions," Sana said, flicking the projector on one of the spare seat screens with a list:

Infraction	Online	IRL
Talking Over	Ten Second Mute	One Second Shock
Mansplaining	Ten Second Mute	One Second Shock

Sindie/Brentry	Twenty Second Mute	One Second Shock
Racism/Sexism/Isms	Sinbin	Random shocks til you fuck off
Talking About Work	Mute until they stop	Intermittent shocks til they stop
Talking About Your Ex	Mute Luci til crying stops	Yeah right
Banging on About No-one Ever Coming IRL to the Pub	N/A	Shock Pól

"Well, that's not fair," Pól said. "Luci, have you seen this?"

Luci sat down, laughing, with her margarita, while Tony got back from his delivery.

"Totally. We agreed the ground rules at the start of the meeting," Luci said, poking her tongue out at him. "Not our fault you were late."

"It's not fucking diversity training, it's Friday drinks." He got another shock. "What was that for?"

"Sorry, not me. I added my rules in earlier, the pub have upgraded their software, let me have a look." Sana fiddled while Tony poured himself a glass of low-alcohol beer - he was still at work.

"If we can make Pól swear, he gets a shock? Awesome. That's worth coming to the pub for."

"Here it is. Recent pubware update, yep - it defaults to shocking swearing. Let me take that off. Fuck, tick. Bollocks, tick - bloody puritanical American software. How do we feel about..." She cut off.

"About what?"

"..." Pól read her lips; she was saying "cunt."

"I think it's real-time blocking you."

"I tried to say, how do you feel about cunt?"

They all did their best dirty laughs.

"Well as someone who works in an STD clinic I only have professional views - OW - about people's sexual organs as I see about a hundred – OW – a week!" Pól yelped as he got shocked repeatedly.

There was now a written rule that they didn't talk about work.

Gathering Power

Stephen Oram

EVERYTHING was neutralised. Her cluster of friends had been hushed. Her connection implants dialled down as close to zero as possible. Her panel displays blurred. She glanced at the fridge, switched off in her determination to avoid an accidental alert to anyone outside of her home. She relished the isolation stretching out in front of her and yet at the same time she longed for someone to break her veneer of solitary contentment. She wanted to be alone and she wanted to be wanted. What someone had once inaccurately nicknamed Schrödinger's Friends.

She sat on her bed flicking her head in rhythmic jerks, moving from one pointless piece of clickbait to the next, and yet despite the attempt to keep the darkness at bay a crippling apathy for life enfolded her. She had a niggling feeling that something was wrong with her cluster buddy Jake, but she pushed it to the back of her mind. She winked, she smiled, and she blew kisses to comments from the online acquaintances she stumbled across in her wanderings. Gestures as pointless as the posts they praised.

There was an irritating thump, thump, thump in the hallway. She wandered to the front door and turned the full-length panel to its viewing setting. The kids were busy bouncing a ball against the wall. They waved. She switched the panel to one-way and watched them for ages. Until she got worried that they would start to appear on her day-to-day connections as proximities, mixed in with her chosen cluster. It was for that very reason that she avoided too much close flesh contact with anyone.

Each one of the implants scattered across her body represented a friend, a member of her cluster. A cluster initially drawn together around a shared obsession with the obscure art movement, Vorticism. She knew who was who from the implant's location and vaguely knew how they were feeling from the pattern of its vibrations. There was a beautiful harmony of frustration and comfort in being constantly aware that they were out there living their lives.

The implant that connected to Jake was still worrying her. He was the only one of her cluster who lived close by and the only one she had flesh-met and he was struggling with something, but she couldn't summon the energy to find out what was wrong. It was selfish, she knew that. It was also about protecting herself from being swamped by whatever he had going on.

Back in her room, she sat and listened to the kids playing in the background. Now she knew what it was, the steady thump of their ball was comforting and their occasional laughter made her smile. She felt more in tune with the world, and when Jake's distress increased another notch, she dialled her panels up to full. He appeared on the nearby street where the windows of the shops selling repurposed tech doubled up as panels. Naked from the waist up, he was swaggering along unashamedly showing off his implants for anyone to see. God, he was sexy. It was brave, it was stupid, and it was typical of Jake. Not the first time, and as ever likely to attract the wrong sort of attention. The display crystallised into a scene created from some of those in her cluster. She loved how it pieced together someone in their kitchen, someone in the street, someone on a train, and so on, into a collage that made it look as if they were all in the same space. Ten of her fifty-strong cluster were waving and shouting greetings.

Jake's distress - or was it excitement? - increased again.

"What's happening with Jake?" she asked.

They ignored her, instead asking how she was, and noting that she'd been absent for a while. Some sent probing messages directly to her earbud asking how she 'really' was and why her vitals were so off, especially her gut bacteria. She told them not to worry and that she'd been getting some alone time, to which they responded with messages of empathy tinged with concern. She was pleased. It was nice to see them again, and soothing to be reminded that they cared. She decided that Jake's distress was most likely a sign of the adrenaline pumping around his body and relaxed into watching his promenade and waiting for the inevitable.

A bunch of anti-cluster thugs appeared and surrounded him, threatening him with scalpels and offering to relieve him of his weirdo implants. He was grinning while dodging from side-to-side. Each time he came into view he yelled for help.

"Shit. Why does he do this?" she muttered.

"Call the police," she shouted.

Her friend Tilly shouted back. "Done."

Imogen screamed at the thugs. "Leave him alone." She told the panel to face-recognise them and within seconds it had displayed their names and addresses. "Look, you stupid idiots," she shouted. "Look at the panel. We know who you are. Piss off, or we will find you and—"

The thugs stopped and stared at the ten faces hurling abuse at them. They turned to each other, hesitated, and then ran away shouting obscenities over their shoulders.

She was exhausted.

Back in bed with her panels blurred she connected directly with a few friends and just chatted. After a few reassuring bouts of banter, she felt better and, propping herself up with her pillows, she set her panels to a half-setting and relaxed. A day of having her cluster nearby without having to interact was what she had wanted, and most likely what she had needed all along.

The doorbell rang. She pulled herself out of bed and ambled to the door. Jake was there, topless, with his big grin and a takeaway. She chuckled; he certainly knew how to press her buttons.

Foundation and Neighbourhood

Benjamin Greenaway

REUBEN'S FIRST day at the Foundation had arrived.

"Welcome, new Social Connectioneer." Hadiza smiled, extending her arms towards him. "Come in, come in. Welcome to MIRSEC. You'll be in with Barney for orientation today, along with our other new joiners. It'll get you a good feel for The Foundation's project, for our big picture, before things get too urgent."

"Right. Yes, of course." Reuben grinned back at her. "Big picture."

"There's such a need for what we have planned here, Reuben. I know you know that. Well, here we are." Hadiza pushed aside the tall glass doors that separated reception from The Foundation's main work area and gestured Reuben inside.

Before him, chatting enthusiastically around a large conference table, centrally positioned in the wide, open plan office space, were MIRSEC's Directory of Commonality, Barney Zepel, co-founder Isaac Ways, and three strangers that Reuben took to be the remaining new hires.

"Welcome, welcome," began Isaac. His voice was the familiar, calm, and sincere fatherly tone behind all of MIRSEC's media presence. "Let's go around the room and find out who we all are."

A relaxed and casual informality was commonplace, almost expected, in platform tech start-ups like The Foundation. The confidence it fosters in new joiners encourages risk-taking during times of rapid development. However, the quality of the assembled talent on show at MIRSEC was far rarer, signalling deep-pocketed, well-motivated investors with schedules to keep.

Between them, Reuben and two of the new hires, Arlo and Jigna, shared five advanced degrees in Applied Game Theory, Machine Learned Informatics, Media and Political Econometrics, and Cyber Psychology. The third, Michel, held two PhDs. And yet they would all begin with at MIRSEC with the same, entry-level title: "Connectioneer".

"I got an actual letter inviting me to a social network once," explained Arlo. "Through the post. An actual, physical letter, with a code on it to scan and download an app."

"What was their premise? Not sustainability, I hope," replied Michel. The group laughed. Arlo pointed back at him, finger on nose, in response.

"Thank you for the levity, Michel," said Isaac, joining the conversation, "but it's an extremely relevant question to our purpose here. If I may ask it again, albeit slightly differently. Can you create community for the sake of having community?"

"Sure you can," replied Michel. "Communities can be found anywhere. Any catalyst subject. Just use the right tools for profile segmentation. Mine them well and tune for engagement and relevancy. Community!"

"How about a time-sharing app? Or a seed and vegetable garden?" suggested Jigna.

"Whatever, could be anything," said Michel. "Well, anything worth selling the lookalike model for at a marketing auction, that is."

Isaac frowned. "Community at MIRSEC is a purpose and an outcome, Michel. Not a marketing strategy. Not an advertising technique. I'm looking for something visceral, something more heartfelt. The Foundation wants Community To Be Real Again. That's why I've brought you all here. That's what I need—what we *all* need you to work on now."

Reuben had heard the slogan a thousand times before. But hearing Isaac repeat it here in this new context of urgency and challenge left him feeling suddenly chilled.

"Barney. Tease the edges off this for them." Isaac gestured to his colleague to take over.

"Sure. What Isaac means, what the difference has to be, is real purpose," Barney began. "I have a friend that role-plays chat in V-Glam. His talent all have fan clubs, their own merchandising, the works. And it's a well-paying gig, as long as he keeps the subscribers engaged. But this one week he has equipment issues, his network goes down. Well, it's a week later, he gets back online and they're all still there! When he reads through the chat logs, sure, initially they were all confused and frustrated. But within hours they had started talking together. Two days later some of them had started to arrange meet ups *in real life*."

"So is MIRSEC's hook to run some kind of self-help group for porn addicts?" Arlo grimaced, visibly confused.

"No hook, Arlo. Nothing like that. We believe that, if we succeed in our mission, spontaneous self-help won't just be confined to the social peripheries!" Isaac clasped his hands together and bowed his head, scanning his assembled dream-team through the tips of his eyelashes.

"What he means, what we're all making the case for here," Barney continued, "is for MIRSEC to facilitate a rejuvenation of personal and civic resilience. A world of individuals strengthened by local connections and common purposes. Not one dissolved and distributed by them and rewired by commercial, supra-governmental sponsors.

"Whatever user experience or content it is that can do that will be the Foundation's content. And we need you to deliver it more seductively than those slot machines of approval you carry with you in your pockets."

The idea certainly appealed to him. But Reuben still couldn't see why anyone would want a platform for training solidarity and empathy through collective, direct action. Research, maybe?

Hadiza interrupted them before he could ask. "Sorry, everyone, but we have an Emergency Weather Warning in effect. And there's a curfew this time too. We'll have to continue this remotely. Brief as it was, so great to see you all here." Beside her, Isaac stood and started to clap. In turn, Barney and Hadiza joined him. And their combined applause lifted the newly formed MIRSEC team from its chairs and back out towards the lobby and the impending alert.

"I still don't buy it, whatever it is," Arlo shrugged.

"It's got to be a trick," Michel replied confidently. "A fake-out for some new brand experience. Allegiance switching is big money, big picture. Real community."

"What if it isn't about the money?" Jigna leant into them both, whispering. "Did either of you hear the rumour about a secret partner funding all of this out of guilt for some shady projects in their past?"

"Nonsense, Jigna. People are too smart for that. They'd see right through any such trick." Arlo fastened down her mask and UV-goggles and stepped outside to face the E.W.W.

Reuben smiled, said his goodbyes, and left to start his walk home. And, as he turned into his street, a cool, twenty minutes ahead of curfew, saw his neighbour approaching from across the road.

"I really should introduce myself at last," he decided. "Although, they look busy. Maybe next time. After all, they've had enough to deal with today already..."

The Valens Program

Jesse Rowell

SHALE OIL extraction below the Sangre de Cristo Mountains unearthed imaginary people in July 2069. People preserved on paper, mostly villains, that never existed. Details of their lives spanned decades in the documents hidden under Valens, an isolated community that had been led by Murphy Vega in the 1960s. For what purpose did he bury his creations, the painted portraits and doctored photographs of a non-existent population?

The Valens Program rose to prominence claiming to have stabilized several small nation-states facing crises a century later. Filing for IPO in 2075, founder Tripp Staveley has never referred to the historic community that shared his trademark, but he has relied on a similar strategy of manufacturing deviants for a targeted audience. Valens' inauspicious beginnings and current success is a cautionary tale as to what could become of our shared reality.

Valens' mission statement, Strengthen to Stabilize, originated from Staveley's time spent in isolation. An unknown illness banished him from his boarding school to his father's New Hampshire estate, where he watched cottontail eat clover outside his bedroom window as he endured years of physical therapy. The idea of incremental improvement through exacting process came to him as he relearned how to walk and mastered archery. After recovering from his illness he used a recurve bow to kill most of the rabbits around his father's estate.

Like all technology startups in the twenty-first century, family money buoyed Tripp's ambitions as he sustained large revenue losses. It wasn't until the antitrust breakup of social media companies that Valens turned profitable, taking over government contracts for countries on the verge of collapse. Staveley remained reticent on his initial success, but much of the credit can be attributed to his AI-constructed deviants.

Referred to internally as the Lotus Server, a reference to the lotus-eaters in Greek mythology, the company created deepfake deviants with family histories and years of social media postings, photos, and videos for communities to examine and vilify. The ghosts that the Lotus Server wove into the fabric of society became so effective as to become hyperreal. People claimed to have known the deepfakes at some point in their lives, gone to school, or worked with them, and above all, hated them.

Murphy Vega had described it a century earlier as hijacking community malice and redirecting it toward ghosts. To assuage discontent in the Valens community in 1962, he deployed his own primitive version of a deepfake after several children contracted plague from prairie dogs. He directed the community's ire toward a travelling salesman who didn't exist, but whom the community blamed for the outbreak and burned in effigy after listening to deceptively edited audio recordings. Stability followed the banishment of the imaginary salesman and he became part of the community's lore.

People are primed to accept deepfakes, Staveley noted in his research, when the campaign aligns to their worldview, political ideologies, or base desires. The Lotus Server aggregates data from consumer behavior and Internet search history to craft a shared valent event that plays on the fallibility of an individual's memories and a community's collective memory. Staveley described it as somebody yelling into a crowd, "Hey, you should all hate this thing over there, okay? Good, now we'll take care of it for you." Spark outrage, offer resolution, and reconcile cognitive dissonance. "Guide an entire community back to health."

Take the curious example of the Birch Bower Incident, named after the clandestine location where lobbyists for the mortuary industry met, a forest of white bark pockmarked with black eyes staring out in all directions. In numerous leaked videos the lobbyists discussed dismantling public health mandates during the 2081 pox pandemic to profit their clients. Roundly condemned by politicians in both parties, legislation quickly passed to increase health measures, saving countless lives, and the lobbyists were publicly shamed. Debate continues to this day as to whether the lobbyists were creations of the Lotus Server, or real people, as some have claimed to have known them or to have been acquainted with distant members of their family.

Staveley has pushed back at the criticism levelled at his company for creating alternate realities, saying, "Who wants a return to illness?" Accomplishing peace in the present by distorting the past justifies the Valens Program, he has asserted, and that communities escaping poverty and violence would agree with him. Staveley has maintained that creating fictitious deviants guarantees that no real people get hurt, and that the Lotus Server is such a small part of the Valens portfolio of business as to not warrant further scrutiny.

All forms of disinformation require scrutiny, academics and researchers counter, even if deployed with altruistic intent. The AI-generated deviants cannot be created devoid of identifiable characteristics like ethnicity, religion, and culture, which has resulted in hate crimes directed at other communities based on the perceived origins of the deviant. When the success of a community is measured by its shared experiences and the open exchange of ideas, then gaslighting and lies become uncontrollable vectors that impede community progress.

Murphy Vega tried to bury his creations under shale and sandstone. The community he once led now lies in ruins, a ghost town of broken boards and wall insulation made of newspaper flaking off like yellow leaves in an autumn wind. The imaginary people he sought to hide from the world live on as objects of derision in a failed social experiment. Tripp Staveley, who has ushered us into the new Valens era, would be wise to learn from the lessons of history - that is, if he can find a history that has not yet been altered.

Accept All Cookies

Liam Hogan

ELAINE'S FINGER hovered over the green button. She'd always been data-wary, part of a generation who went through tediously unclicking sections rather than blindly accepting all – until an AI agent remembered her preferences and managed that for her. But it seemed there was little you could do nowadays without sharing your information, your location, your every desire.

Around her, boxes awaited their unpacking. This was a new beginning, a new life. A semi-retirement, working from her new town home rather than a city office, where most of the interactions were online anyway. Moving out from the big bad for a little more space, and a lot less pressure. Or so the theory went.

The button would hook her into the community net. An all-consuming AI that knew what you owned, what you bought, what problems you had, what skills. And then joined the dots.

Opting out would mean she would be outside of that. Would be as lonely as she had been in the city. Time to be brave. Time for a fresh start.

***

Her doorbell went half an hour later, echoed by a buzz from her watch. A woman stood on the step, a plate held in front of her.

"Hello, neighbour!" she said brightly. "I made cookies. No nuts; I know you're allergic."

"Wow, that's..." Elaine struggled for a moment. Home-made. *Hand*-made. Would they be sanitary? She was up to date with her jabs, but still... it was tempting fate, wasn't it?

The woman, whose name was Jill, chatted on for ten exhausting minutes about the area, places to go walking, or shopping, or drinking, all while Elaine wondered if she should be inviting her in, to the mess.

"But I must let you get on!" Jill said. "Don't worry about the plate, return it when you're settled. Oh! Nearly forgot. I'm at forty-two, with my brood."

Elaine was surprised: forty-two was halfway down the street, a rather distant neighbour. But that was the thing about net communities. With an AI to manage the introductions, they didn't need to be so geographically constrained.

When the gazebo in the garden turned out to be rotten, Mark from halfway across town turned up with his chainsaw, and stayed to help with the job of dismantling the wooden structure. Possibly to make sure the chainsaw wasn't returned blood-spattered, though it had proved remarkably easy – and fun! – to use. All from a throwaway comment on the community page. And when she needed a plumber, recommendations flew in, making the search so much easier. Someone even swung by and picked up all her emptied packing boxes, neatly side-stepping that particular chore.

All very useful, though it felt a little one-way. Jill – who had become a regular visitor, so much so that Elaine updated her calendar to indicate when she was supposed to be working – pointed out that was to be expected when someone new moved in. It took a while to fully integrate.

The community AIs had started as a tool insurers used to lower risk, by sharing feeds from doorcams and watching out for any unusual activity. They'd been co-opted by councils as a way of becoming greener, of reducing waste. Retail businesses had hated them, at first. It meant they sold only the one chainsaw, instead of a half-dozen that sat unused ninety-nine percent of the time. And there had been scandals, early on, over who had access to the data, and who could tweak the feed. But, over time, it had morphed into something more organic, and businesses as well as users had adjusted. To Elaine, it looked like a messenger board, and you didn't see the sophisticated filters that kept it sane, and relevant. When the AI itself reached out, it was always as a gentle prod, a DM with a suggestion, or a no-pressure request.

As autumn arrived Elaine joined a host of her neighbours to pick and share apples and other local crops, and as often as not returned home to find some fresh produce on her doorstop. After an online chat with the horticulturists in the area, she ordered a heritage variety plum tree to sit where the gazebo had once been, an investment in the future.

Christmas, never usually her favourite time of year, was made tolerable by wassailing in the community orchard, by the nods of recognition from neighbours who had become friends, by shared recipes, and shared results. By a waifs-and-strays Boxing Day dinner, a gaggle of good-natured singletons that had led to a half-dozen new friends, and one or two date requests for the New Year.

The local school – also part of the net – offered yoga and other exercise classes in the evenings, for a nominal fee. Far cheaper than the expensive city gyms she'd never really enjoyed, or had time for. Art classes and language classes as well – something to consider for the future.

Elaine volunteered to help out once a month at the Reuse centre, the council-provided containers full of things people no longer wanted, but other people might. Her job was to tag the contents for the net, each re-homing counting towards the council's ambitious recycling targets. She picked up a sturdy bicycle for herself, and registered her electric car on the local pool. She wasn't displeased that others used it more often than she did. Slowly, her life expanded to fill the gaps that perhaps had always been there, hidden behind the hours she'd used to work and her addiction to box sets and Pinot Grigio.

Then, almost a year after she'd moved in, she got a DM from the AI. She went to her window, peered down the street, and clocked the removals van.

"Hello, neighbour!" Elaine said brightly, an hour later, stood on the doorstep under the quizzical gaze of the newest resident and net neighbour. "I made cookies. Gluten free."

Afterword

Yen Ooi

MANY (INCLUDING MYSELF) believe that we are going through a revolutionary period now that is spurned by technological advancements. Some see it as a digital revolution, or an extension of the industrial revolution through technological advancements, while culturally it can be perceived as a participation revolution - a term that social advocate Neil Gibb wrote about in his book of the same title in 2017, but a concept that comparative media professor Henry Jenkins predicted even from the early 1990s in his work surrounding Convergence Culture. Whichever perspective you see this revolution to be from, it can be agreed that digital technology is in its forefront, driving the movement through how we're engaging with the world around us daily, where media participation and consumerism is fully intertwined - where posting and engaging is as crucial as consuming.

But why is this important?

Where there are people there will be communities, and this current revolution is helping change and shape communities that will drive our future.

Communities can be defined as groups of people living in the same place or having a particular characteristic, sharing or having certain attitudes and interests in common. We (humans!) have always been tribal, creating groups with identifiable cultures wherever we might be, and it is because communities are important to us. They have always functioned to provide us with platforms to exercise controlled and shared values, while promoting socialisation through participation, which encourages mutual support of members. Raymond Williams in *Keywords: A Vocabulary of Culture and Society* notes that "What is most important, perhaps, is that unlike all other terms of social organization it [communities] seems never to be used unfavourably, and never to be given any positive opposing or distinguishing term." There isn't an alternative to communities and as social animals (even us introverted ones), we can't live without it, and this will not change as long as communities are still made of people (cue segue to a new discussion on AI communities). But how communities are delivered and accessed by its members in the future will differ according to what kind of future we see.

Working in science fiction often distracts with cool gadgets that tease us with concepts of techtopias and Gibson-esque futures. It is exciting and romantic to dream about these technologically inspired futurescapes, but what these science fictional worlds often ignore - usually in an effort to create more exciting entertainment - is the fact that technology isn't and will never be the main star in our reality. It is a tool to improve our lives, *though autonomous technology does make better stories,* but I digress again. How technology is used to manage, support, and shape communities becomes fascinating, as this starts to bring the future we see (or want to see) into focus.

The stories in this collection touch upon three main areas that technology functions in future communities: social, commercial, and political. We are shown that when left unregulated, things can get overly messy, as in "Disconnect". "Friday Night Drinks at The Horse and Zoom" gives us a fun take on new applications of community rules and tech functions that can be borrowed for more light-hearted and possibly questionable use. "Foundation and Neighbourhood" pokes at the blur between commercial and civic actions of community organisations, while "The Valens Program" paints a darker picture with a story of caution about how hyper-real communities can be created using fake technology to distract and subvert. However, "Gathering Power" and "Accept All Cookies" remind us that ultimately, communities are about connecting people, and whatever way technology helps us get there, we should not forget that connectedness is the ultimate goal.

So, what of the future of communities?

Boringly (for science fiction at least), I believe that communities will remain largely the same, though with new enhancements thanks to technological changes. They will range from local, in-person communities to online groups, and all the in-between hybrid forms. We'll probably get more options in methods of engagement that will be more varied and nuanced but discussing these will only distract us from what is crucial: who are future communities for?

Technology is still an accessory for the privileged, a notion that we've come to ignore as we surpass 5.3 billion unique mobile users globally (GSMA Intelligence[1]) while in comparison 2.4 billion people lack access to adequate food (UN[2]). As the world continues to try and tackle the problem of hunger even when food is deemed a human right, it is understandable that the issue of access to digital technology is brushed aside. After all, remember,

---

1 https://datareportal.com/global-digital-overview#:~:text=There%20are%20 5.31%20billion%20unique,in%20the%20past%2012%20months

2 https://www.un.org/press/en/2021/gashc4336.doc.htm

technology is just a tool. While online connectivity continues to bring people together on a global scale, it also continues to discriminate against those who don't have access to technology and those who aren't able to use technology.

But here comes the interesting bit for science fiction... remember, we are in a revolution! Being in a revolution is ideal for change, and imagination and creativity, which science fiction writers have an abundance of. Being in a revolution is fuel. We can continue this narrative on the future of communities, not with technology as its star, but with the rightful membership. People. And if we are going through a participation revolution, then who *isn't* participating matters. How we ensure that communities work for their people while improving accessibility matters even more. I believe that we have the capacity to drive this revolution into a future that includes all forms of communities, without discrimination. And if that future can be laced with some cool tech or is set in space, even better.

PART 4:
The Digitisation
of Central Money

The Accountant

Sophie Sparham

"TELL ME AGAIN what you want," I said, cracking my fingers.

Denis squirmed in his seat, twisting his hat in his hands. "I need the sex credits bringing down," he said, "and the alcohol ones." One lamp lit the dark room. I had positioned it in his direction to keep myself in shadow. In the cone of light, I could see the beads of sweat on his face.

"What's your code?" I asked.

"Five-five-four-seven-eight-six," he replied.

I typed the numbers onto my screen and almost spat my coffee. "Two hundred sex credits this month?"

Denis hung his head and I felt the pit of my stomach drop. Sometimes it was hard to tell who you were dealing with. Who cared as long as they paid?

"I took out a few magazine subscriptions," he shrugged, "visits to Coco's. It's been a month since the wife left ..."

"I don't care," I stopped him. I looked at his health credits, which were considerably lower. I transferred fifty over. Moved another fifty to home credits and transportation. He sat there in silence as I went through the bank statement, added a few weekend trips, a fake gym membership, art classes. Finally, I sat back and sipped at my coffee.

"That should do you," I said.

"Really?" He beamed.

"Really," I replied. "When's the job interview?"

"Next week."

"Consider your credit test passed."

Denis stood up. "Oh, thank you!"

He held out his hand. I didn't take it.

"You can go now." I gestured to the door.

I always waited fifteen minutes after every client left. I tapped my watch, waited until the hand struck one before putting on my trench coat and stepping out into the darkness. Outside, the first signs of autumn littered the street. Dead leaves crunched beneath my boots as I crossed the road and made my way through the park. Something caught my eye. It was small and silver and shone dimly in the light. I bent down, ran my fingers over it. How the hell had it got here? I hadn't seen a coin in over ten years. Not since the system went total digital.

I shivered, thinking back to the leather purse I used to carry in my left pocket, a time before the days of digital monitoring. A time when you could walk into a bar without having to turn your balance into alcohol credits, where your gym membership didn't count towards your health score, when bank statements weren't checked like passports. A time when I had a job. One that was above-board. There were few of us left now. Most had retrained or been sucked into *Monetor*, the financial monitoring conglomerate. I put the coin into my pocket and squoze it tight, stepping back onto the street. The wind picked up and I hitched my scarf around my neck, crossing the road. My pager beeped. I pulled it from my pocket. This was the only way me and Akeel were able to keep in contact without them tracking us.

New job.

Akeel, I typed, *it's late.*

New job. Keep walking.

A shiver ran down my spine. I turned around. The street was empty. I walked faster, damning my heels as they clicked against the concrete. A woman was stood on the corner. She lowered her hood as I approached.

"The Accountant, I take it?" she asked.

I remained silent.

She had straight black hair and olive skin, a mole just above her lip on the right side. A sweet smell drifted from her, like cheap strawberry perfume, the kind you wore at school to impress boys.

"Did you get the message?"

"I don't know what you're talking about," I said. *She'd intercepted my pager. How?*

She handed me a credit statement. *My* credit statement, before the edits I'd performed. My hairs stood up as I stared down at my real name.

"Where did you get this?" I asked.

She smiled. "I'll walk with you to the train tracks."

The woman looked me up and down as we walked. "I thought you'd be ..."

"A man," I finished her sentence.

"Blonde," she corrected me.

I ran my hand through my ginger bob. I'd always prided myself on keeping my red hair.

"Did you like the coin?" she asked. "Took us a while to find a collector, we thought it'd remind you of the good old times."

"Who are you?"

"A friend." She offered me a cigarette. I shook my head and she lit her own. "You're a difficult person to find," she said.

"I try and keep myself offline," I admitted. Harder done than said in a world that no longer had paper money.

113

"We've got a job for you," the woman continued.

"We?"

"Me and my employer," she said, taking a drag. "We need you to change the credit history of Alva Damn."

I took a sharp intake of breath. Damn was one of the candidates running in the elections to lead the Strive Party. A little too Mother Teresa for me, but I could get on board with her.

"Are you sure?" I asked.

"We're quite sure." The woman threw her bud to the floor.

"I don't really …"

"Don't get all charity case on me, you just cleared that pervert's record."

My cheeks flushed. How long had they been watching me?

"That's different," I said.

"How?" the woman asked.

I paused.

She smiled. "There will of course be a fee."

"How much?"

"Sixty thousand credits."

I tried to keep my features neutral.

"Pretty good for only a few minutes work?" She paused. "I'll leave it with you." She put a hand on my shoulder, before turning and walking back down the street. I leant against the boarded-up newsagent and caught my breath. Half a woman's face smiled down at me on the peeling billboard across the road. The old railway stretched out into the distance. I climbed onto the bridge and walked into darkness, away from the metropolis. Alva Damn was a politician, but not a monster. It was difficult to say if she was one of the good guys. I didn't believe in good guys. '...*you just cleared that pervert's record ...*' My new *friend* was right and I hadn't even thought twice about it.

The Summoned

Eva Pascoe

THE BELL at GASDAQ (Gamers Association of Security Dealers and Quotations) rang loudly, as young CEO Rico Nada raised his hands and clapped at the SmoothCat Software team. "Thanks to these guys, we have accomplished the impossible. I couldn't ask for a better crew to share my journey," hollered Rico at the top of his voice as the ticker tape showed Smoothcat's shares going well above the launch price.

Carmen, his mom, was peeking from behind his team. She was relieved that Rico's audacious IPO, with only small revenues, had reached twenty-two Alphas per share, valuing the company at thirteen billion. SmoothCat's code was a breakthrough, lifting Alphaverse gaming for everyone to a new comfort level, with no dropped frames or incorrect GPU frame-pacing, making virtual worlds possible for all, not just the hard-core gamers.

It was a long journey for Rico Nada. GASDAQ was a closed shop. Only the Summoned had been allowed to tap the market for innovation funds. Known as the Tall Men, The Summoned had a monopoly on access to Alphas' money. Outliers like Rico Nada were not invited. Born on the wrong side of the tracks, Rico was the son of a single mom, a cleaner at Ivy Academy, where the Tall Men send their sons. The story was that they came from the east, on their big boats, many centuries ago. They brought their own currency, called Alpha, and quickly monopolised business funding.

They never failed, their deals always worked out, and fortunes were made due to the special capability that Tall Men brought with them from the east with their enhanced money-making gift, which they absorbed from an ivy plant. It was a type of ivy that surrounded them at the Academy for four years. It spread a type of virus that, if absorbed for those four years, ensured a high level of viral load and gave Tall Men an instinct to de-risk financial decisions to zero.

With time, they became the sole handlers of new funding and banking. Their wealth grew rapidly as they concentrated their Alpha currency and became owners of all real estate. Then, the Summoned extracted fees from the people for access to anything from housing to transport, even digital worlds like the game platform Alphaverse. Tall Street Journal, where Tall Men's wives worked, praised their wins, reinforcing the idea of Tall Men's "magic" financial powers. It was a perfect setup that worked for centuries as the rich grew richer.

The rest of the people fell into poverty, unable to save to acquire assets or borrow money for housing, trapped in skyrocketing rents and poorly paid gig jobs. The poor were only allowed small tokens for Alphaverse for a few hours of gameplay. Tall Men kept the population occupied.

Against all odds, Rico found a way in. Home-schooled by Carmen, he developed his love of making games and coding late into the night, surrounded by the scent of ivy. His bedroom was decorated with ivy leaves that Carmen would steal from the Academy, smuggling out a few fresh branches at a time. With the ivy, Carmen made sure that her only son had the same chances with Alpha's money gift as the Tall Men's sons.

When Rico Nada was seven, Carmen told him that his father was a student at the Ivy Academy. "He was tall and good looking, that is all I can tell you. That is why you are tall, you are in part a Tall Man." Rico grew with the conviction that he too could succeed. He pushed through to get funds for his game tech - something that nobody beyond The Summoned could dream about.

His gaming buddies chipped in from their gig-jobs income to fund his ideas for SmoothCat. The team was camping in Carmen's tiny apartment behind the Academy where Rick's code was developed with funding from players, independent of the big backers. Rico realised: he could turn the tables on the Tall Men.

SmoothCat made any metaverse smooth, taking the power away from Alphaverse owners. Any wins in any universe were accumulated in CatCoins and transferable between games. Players could leverage assets in one game to borrow for a new homestead in another. Their assets grew quickly. CatCoins were so convenient for gamers that they became a widely-used currency.

New game startups could use their earned CatCoins from one game as collateral for their own metaworld. And, after twelve months, Rico got to raise his hand in triumph at the GASDAQ podium.

Descending the podium behind him, Carmen's happy expression began to change. She opened her handbag, taking out a photograph. "Take a look at this." She handed it over to Rico.

The photo showed a young, very tall man, standing next to a waterfall in the lush mountains. There was something familiar about his smile.

"It is your father," said Carmen quietly. Rico looked at her surprised. "I thought he was one of the Tall Men students?"

"Rico Nada, your dad was not one of those Summoned fakes here," she said dismissively. "Your father was the real Summoned - my childhood sweetheart from back home, from the tallest tribe in the south, Quinamo, meaning "The Summoned". He played basketball for the village team but he was gunned down defending his younger brother from drug dealers. I escaped up north, getting a janitor job at the Ivy Academy."

Rico asked, "Why are you telling me this now?"

"I wanted you to know that you did it all by yourself. That you succeeded without being one of them."

"Was it the ivy in my room? Isn't it why the Tall Man are so money-savvy?" asked Rico.

"It is just a ruse to persuade others about the mystery surrounding the Tall Men, a trick they play on us to justify their stratospherically high salaries, banking fees, exclusive control over Alphas.

"I found a paper from the last century under the bed of the Ivy Academy Dean – it described the Ivy story origins, the creation of 'super credentials,' to make them look infallible. The truth is it's just a fable. I put the ivy in your room, so you felt confident too.

"The finance companies on the Tall Street only recruit for risk capital and banks from the Ivy Academy, so nobody ever found out that outsiders can be good with money too. The truth is that your coding skills didn't get better just because you sniffed your ivy for four years." She giggled.

Rico raised his eyes and saw the giant GASDAQ tickertape running his stock ticker. It was going up. He smiled. He liked the idea of being a Quinamo, an ancient tribe famous for tall men, top traders before the fake Summoned arrived in their big boats.

Quinamo owned property as a collective. "We will share this with others," Rico decided. "CatCoins will be a DAO-owned venture, everyone will participate in the success and grow our capital.

Your destiny was to break the Tall Men monopoly on Alphas." Carmen looked at him with pride. "You and your gaming crew are the real Summoned. Bring on the CatCoin revolution!"

Failing Fathers

Stephen Oram

"I DON'T want to beg, but we are best mates 'n' all that."

"You have to be kidding. They'll trace it so easily, and then where will we be?"

I shrugged and carried on tinkering with the code of the car that had been brought in to have its latest patches installed. I wasn't paying proper attention to what I was doing, but then if they couldn't pay me a decent wage why should I?

I tried again, speaking loudly but not directly to him. "I have to buy food *and* heat the house *and* it's the wife's birthday. All I want is for you to do some shopping for me. I'll pay you back straight away. I don't see how they'll know it's for me and not you."

"You've heard the rumours. Anything that smacks of reparation avoidance is swiftly dealt with. Shame laundering, isn't that what they call it?"

I kept my eyes firmly fixed on the screen in front of me, trying not to make a big deal out of it. Even though it was.

"It's only one weekly food shop."

"Apart from the illegal bit, your lineage owes my lineage and until that's done…"

He had a point, but he was wrong. It wasn't my forefathers who stole stuff from other countries and locked it away in the British Museum.

I stared at him. "That genetic profiling is crap. Completely ignores the fact that those elite fuckers were stealing from my sort at the same time as robbing the heritage of yours."

He mumbled something I couldn't make out.

"It's too generic. It should be a class thing, not a country thing. No way does it trace those who were really responsible."

Another mumble.

I looked away. "Still, we are where we are, as my mother used to say. For better or worse we have programmable money and it has rules."

He came and stood next to me. "You're my friend. I get that. And, that's why I know we'll rise above this whole reparation thing. It only lasts until it's all paid back."

I nodded, unable to reply. He just didn't get it.

"Not the sins of my fathers," was all I could mutter under my breath. I was innocent. My whole family line was innocent and yet my Heritage Pound was worth less than his because the cost of re-balancing the abuses of other people's ancestors fell to me and mine.

I carried on speaking while working. "I wasn't asked about the British Museum being privatised. I wasn't consulted about the contents becoming the asset behind the most widely-used private currency. It wasn't my decision to give it favourable interest rates and lower tax rates than the other currencies. It's those bastards in charge of the Bank of England's digital currency." I rubbed my temples and sighed. "I agree with the government offsetting the reparation obligations of its colonial past, but there's a world of difference between agreeing with the what, and agreeing with the how."

He tutted and went back to his bench.

We ignored each other for the rest of the day, but as he left he called across. "I'll see if the kids have any ideas."

My teenage daughter met me outside, determined that I should buy her mother a birthday present.

"Just a small one," she said.

I told her we couldn't afford it and that her mother understood, but she insisted.

"Why don't we use a different currency? One that works for us, not against us. Then we could afford it," she said.

I explained as best I could about how difficult it was to be accepted by any other currency because their rules of interaction with the CBDC were predicated on how risky their customer base was, and we were in one of the highest risk brackets.

She pushed hard. "Why not do what Sasha's dad does? He owns shares in art that's worth more and more every day. Non. Fungible. Tokens. Get it?"

Fine for him, I explained, but we don't have the capital to begin with. She huffed and puffed, throwing one superficially thought-through solution after another at me. It was as if she considered me to be stupid. As if she thought I'd not explored all these options. In my head at least.

She made that disgusting sound with her tongue. "It's crap."

"I know," I said. "You're right. It's the very people whose ancestors were responsible for the appalling past of our country who use the other currencies. They escape *any* consequences of the national reparation."

She was fuming and with the familiar cry of every teenager, she pointed out that it wasn't fair. All I could do was agree with her. Replying with the age-old parental response that life just isn't fair.

It was an unsatisfying exchange for both of us.

My mate was chatting to me the next day and I was telling him all about it, and despite the seriousness of the situation I found myself laughing along with him about the idealism of youth. We reminisced about our own teenage years and how we'd been certain that we knew how the world worked, and how it could be a lot better. It was good to be back on jovial terms and he was trying to tell me something his daughter had said, but talking about our kids behind their back was making me feel uncomfortable.

I ignored him, until he came and stood by me with a big grin on his face. "Here, give me your phone," he said, grabbing it from my bench.

I frowned, but with curiosity. He swiped the screen and then held his own close to it.

"There," he said. "You'll never guess what. My daughter's been using her Heritage Pound advantage to invest in that new youth currency. Know the one? She's made a mint out of limited-edition skins in those games she's fixated with. And… wait for it… she wants to gift your family some shares." With a thumbs-up he added, "It's allowed."

I was speechless. What a brilliant mate, and what a great father.

Heartbeat

Wendy M. Grossman

THE FIRST disaster was the unambiguous pink line. The second was the little red light that began flickering. Her positive result was being transmitted to the Texas Department of Health. In her haste and anxiety, she had forgotten to throw the pregnancy test in the microwave and zap the chip. She banged on the test hopelessly with her fist. The light turned green to signal the data transfer was complete.

The third disaster came a week later, when the doctor showed her the ultrasound image and said, "There's a heartbeat."

She stared at him, dismayed. "There *can't* be."

He looked down at his notes. "It's sooner than I'd have expected, given what you've told me," he said. "But....it's very definite."

She felt frozen. He waited, making notes.

She finally croaked out in a near-whisper: "Do I have options?"

"I can give you a list of pregnancy support organisations," he said. "And some adoption agencies. Though a lot of them have waiting lists."

"For people who want babies?"

"No, for mothers like you, who are looking for adoptive parents."

Mother. She felt sick. "I can't do this," she said in despair.

He shook his head. "I can't help you any further. It's illegal. And they watch me all the time. I'll email you a copy of the scan. You can get dressed now. Take all the time you need."

At reception, on her way out, the nurse gave her a prescription for pre-natal vitamins and the lists the doctor had mentioned. She stared at them, trying to make sense. Then the nurse coughed a little and said something that sounded like a web address.

"What?"

Again, barely audible.

She reached for a pen to write it down on one of the lists.

"No!" the nurse hissed sharply. "Don't write it down. Don't use your phone. Use a computer. Not at the library or university. Don't use Google. Use an anonymous proxy in another country. The Netherlands, Ireland, somewhere. They'll help you find something."

She repeated the address quietly.

It took her two days to work up the nerve to access it. She learned a lot during that time. She learned, for example, that her payments were blocked so neither airlines, nor Amtrak, nor Greyhound would sell her a ticket to anywhere out of state, she couldn't buy alcohol, and all her receipts carried printed nutrition advice. She could travel to near the state line, but Uber and Lyft wouldn't take her across. She was six months too young to rent a car, and smart road pricing meant every mile in her own car would be logged. Even her cryptocurrency wallet refused to open to pay for chorizo from a taco truck.

"I can't take the risk," the taco seller said. "My chorizo is perfect. But if you miscarry, someone could sue me and claim I helped you get an abortion. How do I prove I didn't?"

She had told no one she was pregnant. Everyone she didn't know knew she was. Everyone she really knew had no idea.

Finally, she used DuckDuckGo to find an anonymous proxy in Russia and logged onto an Irish help site. "We know how you feel because Texas now is Ireland not long ago," the FAQ began. Through the site, she found lists of out-of-state clinics and sites that would send pills.

She'd already established that no one would risk the liability of helping her get to a clinic - if payment intermediaries and travel companies wouldn't risk liability, she couldn't burden friends. It would have to be mail-order pills. And she'd have to pay with something like anonymous cash.

"It's not going through," said the post office clerk when she tried to buy a money order in US dollars with her bank debit card.

"Why?"

The clerk looked at her screen. "It says here, 'Abortion risk'."

She wanted to sob. "What am I going to do?" she wailed.

"I can't help you," the clerk said. A frozen, miserable pause. "You need cash. US dollars, not Texas dollars. Then you can buy a money order."

She hadn't seen US dollars in years. Her payment systems did all necessary conversions automatically, ever since a governor had fulfilled his election campaign promise and converted all in-state payments to Texas dollars. It was part of a plan to "keep money local" and "defund the blue states." Even in Austin, ATMs didn't dispense US dollars anymore.

"How?" she said.

"Get cash here. Then go to the Cambio. The foreign exchange. Down that way. Ask any Latino on the street, they'll know. You'll find it."

It was a two-mile walk to the Cambio, which was in an old video game arcade and seemed to serve immigrants sending money home. She studied the machines: some sent bitcoin and other cryptocurrencies around the world. Several accepted only Mexican pesos; a few others accepted Texas dollars but only to send to various foreign countries. Finally she found it: Texas dollars to US dollars, cash to cash. The machine was dark. Her knees buckled and she found herself sitting on the floor in front of it, crying.

Someone was coming from out of the back. She grabbed some Kleenex out of her bag and scrabbled inside it, trying to look calm, like she'd just sat down for a minute to use her phone... until she remembered she'd left it at home, to avoid its tracking.

It was an older woman.

"The machine is broken," she said.

The woman knelt down and reached around behind it. It began booting up. "Turned off," she said. "Mistake. Ten minutes." She looked at the opened purse, the Kleenex, the spilled contents, the tear-stained face, and seemed to understand the situation. "You will be all right."

The day after it was done, she looked at the doctor's emailed scan in her inbox. She paused with her finger on Delete. *I should have some record,* she thought. This really happened. She would need the reminder, to keep her rage fresh for the coming campaign. She followed the steps to make an NFT, and saved it to a tiny USB stick, and only then deleted the original.

Where to keep it - out of sight, but not out of mind? She dropped it inside one of the towers of the Lego Hogwarts castle her ex-boyfriend had left behind. One day, she thought, the law would change, and on that day she would smash it with a base-ball bat.

The Money Talk

Paul Currion

"Heeeeeeeeeeeey," says Money, "Why aren't you out there spending?"

"How long do I have left?" I ask her.

"I am sorry to say," says Money, "the value of your Basic will halve in less than a day."

"I hate Basic," I sigh. Basic is so basic, it's embarrassing to be seen on an exchange with it. Even Money's tone gets sneery when I ask her to spend it.

"But the longer you leave it," says Money, "the less it's worth. And that makes me unhappy."

I yearn for a post-Money future. I tried several creator gigs but got swallowed by the long tail every time. My last try was launching an online course on how to develop online courses, until the platform changed their conditions so that creators could only pay each other in course credits. Money suggested that I take a guitar course, which I gave up after a month.

My parentals will happily keep hiring me from RelEx - unless a better offer comes in, which is unlikely because I have no gig, my Basic is about to halve in value, and I still can't play guitar. After I turn fifteen, their payments turn optional, but they aren't just rentals, they're also my real parents. We love each other, but love has a price: the ambient suspicion that I'm just not worth it.

"Let's get some Grub!" suggests Money, who is everywhere. As I pull my £TEX jacket on, Money is in the fibres; as I slam the SeeCure door, Money is in the alarm system; as I stumble to Grubstore, Money is steering us through the dark forest of contracts and counter-bids that make up the world.

I stole that last line from the Post-Money Manifesto, which was worth every PolitiCoin I paid for it. Stephanie Zimm made so much PolitiCoin from publishing it that she was able to buy a seat in Parliament. (I ask Money to remind me to vote in the nearest quadratic election; I'm running low on PolitiCoin and I need to get paid.)

Now Stephanie Zimm gets paid in Westminsters, which may as well be Post-Money. Good for her, that's what I say. I even have the first line of her Manifesto hashed in my Money sig: "How would I live without the Smart Shades of Money to stop my Eyes being gouged by the Harsh Reality underneath This World?"

Mostly Money stays in the background until she's needed, and then she becomes my best friend. "Are you ready to eat?" asks Money. "Grubstore special offer on falafel sandwich. You advertise them for a day, they pay you in falafel."

"Haggle," I tell Money. "A full day is too much. I don't want to get banned from a club tonight just 'cause it's sponsored by one of Grubstore's competitors." Money haggles on my behalf and settles on a half-day, and the Grubstore logo shimmers onto my £TEX sleeve. It's horrible but I smile at the store clerk as I bite into the falafel sandwich. He smiles back as I break a tooth on something round and rock-like.

Lucky me. I've been saving my CursePurse for weeks, so I spend freely; a savage stream of Curses that knocks Grubstore's reputation value on several exchanges. The clerk is still smiling for some reason. Out of my mouth I pull one actual gold coin with a pretty lady's profile on it, and I can't believe it.

I'm holding in my hand a Meg.

"Congratulations!" says the clerk.

"Give me the Meg!" says Money.

"What the fuck?" I sputter as a broken tooth comes loose.

"You've won our Lifetime Lottery!" says the clerk.

"Establish ownership!" shouts Money, but I turn down her volume so I can think. A Meg is - a Meg is post-Money. A Meg means value everywhere. A Meg is the KYC jelly that will let me slide into one of the big exchanges, where your word is your currency. Where people take you seriously when you tell them you're not interested.

Still, I'm not thinking straight. "I'll sue you!" I tell the clerk while I instruct Money to put a legal token, any legal token, in escrow to show him I'm serious.

"You can't sue us," says the clerk, listening to his own Money carefully, "without voiding the terms of the Lifetime Lottery."

He conspiracies in my direction, but I hold up the falafel sandwich like a gun. "Try to take this off me," I tell him, "and the Cop Shop is going to serve you some truncheon on an hourly rate that I decide."

I turn Money back up and let her establish ownership of the Meg on-chain. I drop the falafel sandwich on the floor and walk out the door. A bunch of busy bees have heard the news and hum towards me, most already livestreaming, Money hearing their exclusive offers so I don't even have to deal with them.

And that's when I realise - I don't need their exclusive offers anymore. I have a Meg. I instruct Money to turn down all of their offers. But I'm not even sure I need Money anymore. That feeling you get when you stand up too fast after sitting down for too long, that's what this feels like.

I sprint home - earning FitPoints every time my trainers hit the pavement, but why should I even care about FitPoints anymore either? - but not even I can run faster than the news, which travels as fast as people will pay it to. My parentals are already waiting outside as I rush up.

"Doesn't this change everything?" I ask them. A life without Money. I can't even imagine. Where will her voice in my head go, now that I no longer need to truck and barter?

"It doesn't change the most important thing," my mother replies, as my father smiles proudly and takes my hand, but RelEx is already pinging Money to ask me if I want to buy out their parental contract. Love and worry, respect and guilt, none of it stored in a ledger, and suddenly I feel more alone than I can stand.

Slow Money

Vaughan Stanger

"TONIGHT ON the Rho Malik Show I'm talking to the brains behind Gaia Bank – slogan: *Slow money to save the world* – which launches its highly anticipated range of eco-friendly financial services today. In the studio, we have eco-entrepreneur Lise Sottomayer, while Deep Green guru Michael Olunga joins us from cyberspace. Welcome, both!"

"Hi!"

"Hi from Deep Green!"

(Rho frowns then turns to Lise.) "So, Lise, for the benefit of our audience, please explain how slow money works."

(Lise smiles.) "Okay, but first, let's roll back to December 2020. I was looking for ecologically sound enterprises to invest in when I found an article about a tree banking project in Kerala State, in India. The local community planted saplings, and after three years its residents mortgaged each tree for an interest-free loan renewable annually for ten years. If the tree wasn't chopped down, the loan never needed repaying. Meanwhile, the community harvested the trees' fruit and seeds. It was an ecological win-win-win, benefitting the individual, the community, *and* the environment. Three months later, I established my own version in Epping Forest."

(Rho frowns.) "But what happens if a mature mortgage tree dies before the loan expires?"

"We transfer the loan to another tree, usually an offspring. This worked *very* well."

"So why did you need Michael?"

"After about a year, we observed some odd behaviours, such as neighbours of trees that'd been chopped down dropping unripe fruit or sterile seeds."

(Rho waggles a forefinger.) "So the remaining trees were signalling their disapproval?"

(Lise nods.) "Yes, exactly! I'd read somewhere that trees exchanged information. I wondered whether I could optimise my tree bank's productivity if I could understand their messages. When I heard about Michael's Deep Green project, I contacted him immediately."

(Rho turns to him.) "Michael, how did you feel about Lise's business ambitions?"

"I thought, hey, here's a potential new source of funding!" *(Laughs.)* "Seriously though, Lise's tree bank offered the perfect opportunity to apply Deep Green in a real-world scenario."

"Deep Green is an AI, right?"

"Yes."

"How on Earth can an AI communicate with trees?"

"Because of what's *under* the earth. As Lise said, we already knew that trees communicate. They do that using an underground fungal network."

(Rho sighs.) "I feel a science lesson coming on…"

"Then I'll keep it brief. Trees receive nutrients from the fungi situated within and around their roots. In return, the trees transfer sugars *to* the fungi. It's a fully functional network, with messaging and transfer of resources."

"The trees' network runs on sugar?"

"In essence."

(Rho chuckles) "Sweet!"

(Michael groans.)

(Rho continues.) "Seriously though, how did Deep Green learn their language?"

"I embedded nano-sensors throughout Lise's trees and their fungus. Deep Green monitored the quantity and concentrations of sugars transported around the network while Lise's robots conducted routine tasks like harvesting and pruning. But when they chopped down a healthy mature tree, Deep Green really got the message! Soon, we had the syntax, ontology and the—"

"Ontology?"

"The collection of concepts describing the world. What the trees know about, in effect. We discovered they understand the concepts of value, of lending and borrowing, even of charity. Individually and collectively, they know how to value resources, and how that value changes over time. In truth, they understand how to manage resources far better than humanity does. Lise thought we should solicit their help."

(Lise interjects.) "The real breakthrough came when Michael worked out how to send messages the trees could read. That's when we learned they'd been trying to message Deep Green! Anyway, now we had two-way communications going, albeit *slowly*, I proposed using Deep Green as an interface between humanity and sources of ecologically sustainable finance. Three years on and Gaia Bank is the outcome. It incorporates my company, Michael's Deep Green, and a bunch of new AIs. Gaia Bank offers a full range of long-term saving plans and loans, which, unlike those based on traditional banking, or worse, crypto-credit, will benefit the customer *and* the planet."

"Very cute!" *(Rho turns to Michael.)* "But Michael, there are still a couple of things I don't understand."

"Hopefully, Deep Green can help."

"Ah, you see, but that's my point. I get how Lise's tree bank works, also how it'd work even better using Deep Green. I sort-of get how the forests could set interest rates and terms, so humanity's need for finance doesn't end up destroying them. But here's the thing: *Gaia* isn't just trees and forests. Even a desert is an ecosystem. So Gaia Bank must value everything living in, on, under, or flying above the Earth. But how does a desert value itself, or even know that it should? Never mind how it tells anyone!"

"Happily, we can exploit our experience with Deep Green."

(Rho frowns.) "How does that help?"

"The forests interact with every other ecosystem, whether directly or indirectly. They can value a desert for us. My team has constructed new AIs to simulate financial trading with every major ecosystem. Hence, Deep Silver, Deep Blue, Deep—"

"Ah, so Gaia Bank is a portfolio of simulations run by *artificial* intelligences which talk to trees!"

"To be accurate, Deep Green is now a *natural* intelligence."

"Do you mean the forests are running Deep Green?"

(Michael chuckles.) "No, the forests *are* Deep Green."

(Rho turns to the audience.) "So, there you have it, folks: bank with Gaia and the trees will be in charge of *all* your money!"

(Michael frowns.) "It's not *quite* as simple as that. You see, the AIs—"

(Rho waggles his forefinger.) "Which brings us to the second thing I don't understand. *(He turns to Lise.)* "You see, Lise, I'm *still* not sure whether Gaia Bank is the real deal. Some aspects are, obviously. *You*, Lise, are real. Your mortgage trees are real. *(He turns back to Michael.)* But Michael, are *you* real?"

(Michael smiles.) "Real enough to interview."

(Rho frowns.) "In which case, please tell everyone whose interests you represent."

"I represent Gaia Bank, of course."

"Which is a collection of AIs running simulations. So I have to ask whether you—"

"I am what Gaia Bank needs me to be."

(Rho nods.) "Uh-huh." *(He turns to Lise.)*

"Lise, do you have a take-home for our audience?"

"Rho, what everyone needs to know is that Gaia Bank provides ecologically sound financial products for the long term."

(Rho sighs.) "Ironically, we're out of time, so on that note—"

(Michael chuckles.) "But not a *bank* note."

"Ha! Very good. Okay, I'll *leaf* the last message to, erm, 'Michael Olunga'."

(Michael groans, then holds his arms out like a messiah.) "For your great-grandchildren's sakes: bank with Gaia to save the world. That's the message."

(Rho stands, addressing the audience.) "Happily for us, it's a sugar-coated one… I think."

Afterword
David G.W. Birch

I WAS RATHER surprised to see that when Boba Fett was receiving tribute in his magnificent palace on the planet of Tatooine that the supplicants arrived with chests full of coins. This seemed to me a strange vision of money in a world of hyperspeed, light sabres, and antigravity landspeeders. I mean, come on, if you can send data through wormholes and harness the energy of suns, you'd surely be mining bitcoin or Bobacoin or ForceCash or whatever.

I shouldn't be too critical, I suppose. It's hard to think about the future of anything, given the nature of intertwined technological and cultural evolution that could take us in so many different directions, but money poses a particular problem. We tend to think of money as a law of nature, rather than the rather temporary set of institutional arrangements that it actually is. The former Governor of the Bank of England, Mervyn King, wrote about this in his book *The End of Alchemy*, pointing out that central banks have not been around for a terribly long time and there's no reason to imagine that they will continue to the heat death of the universe.

Insofar as people actually spend any time thinking about what money is, their view dates from what I'm tempted to call the "Golden Century" where the gold standard overlapped with electronic communications to create hard money that could travel faster than a speeding person. In my book *Before Babylon, Beyond Bitcoin,* I date this precisely from 1871 and the beginning of electronic funds transfer services to 1971 and Richard Nixon's decision to end the convertibility of the US dollar into gold.

(I remember attending a seminar at Chatham House, the UK foreign policy think tank, a few years ago, and being asked a question by a well-educated and experienced journalist which made it clear that she thought that the ten-pound note in her wallet was somehow backed by gold in the Bank of England. This hasn't been true for generations, and yet it remains the basic scaffolding of the prevailing paradigm.)

The idea that the money that we have in our wallets is ultimately backed by some sort of valuable and scarce commodity is deeply rooted. That's why we need artists and writers to imagine future conceptions of money that go far beyond an extrapolation of bitcoin to the point where it is using half of all the energy in the known universe, or a version of a scarce commodity (for example, gold-pressed latinum in Star Trek), and why I so greatly appreciated the opportunity to take part in the "Tales from the Cybersalon" series.

From my experiences running the Future of Money Design Award for a few years (an award specifically for artists creating visions of the different aspects of the future of money), I knew that these artistic visions would be far more interesting than the sort of techno-deterministic chrome-washing of current prejudices that people like me come up with. If you had asked me to write a story about the future of money in 1690, would I have imagined a gold standard? A Bank of England? Paper money as a circulating means of exchange?

I won't spoil your experience of the works by giving away any of the storylines, but I will say that the imagination shown by Sophie Sparham in "The Accountant" (surely a Netflix series in the making, an *Ozark* for the NFT age), the connection between communities and emotions set out by Paul Curton in "The Money Talk", the intertwining of fungibility and family that Stephen Oram explores in "Failing Fathers" (Narayan Kocherlakota, of the Federal Reserve Bank of Minneapolis, once famously observed that "money is a primitive form of memory"), Eva Pascoe's implicit call for revolution in "The Summoned", Wendy Grossman's nightmare vision of a connected future that links health data to payments data, and Vaughan Stanger's return-to-nature tale of future computing made the experience stimulating, worthwhile, and above all, fun. I hope that you will enjoy them as much as I did.

(The stories also added to my vocabulary. For example, the phrase "KYC jelly" is now indelibly marked in my memory.)

What these stories had in common was that they were not so much about how the money of the future would work, but what it would do to us and our relationships. I like being challenged to think about this because, as is often said, we tend to overestimate the short-term impact of new technology (cf, self-driving cars) but completely underestimate the long-term impact of new technology (cf, MySpace).

You might argue that in light of recent events there may be many more people in the world searching for means of exchange beyond using US dollars or even bitcoin but it seems to me more likely that in the future, money as we know it will simply disappear. Money is an intermediary. As Marshall McLuhan said, it's a specialist technology. We use money as a common means of exchange so that we don't have to find someone who wants our creative writing skills in exchange for a chicken. But finding that coincidence of wants in a future universe where everything is connected to everything else, all of the time, is a trivial matter.

By the way, before you start tweeting about the Gold Standard, or cryptocurrency or faster-than-light payments, note that right now the Taliban are paying Iran using not dollars, not bitcoin, but water. They have opened the Kamal Khan dam to release water for the Iranians to pay them back for sponsoring terrorist groups in Helmand. A Water Standard looks more likely in the fifty-degree future of the world than a gold standard or bitcoin. Truth is always stranger than fiction.

Postface - Writing the Tales

Dr Christine Aicardi

HOLD ON BEFORE closing this volume. Spare me a few minutes, and you may start understanding why the authors who have contributed short near-future science fiction stories to this volume, came to write them in the first place. I had the privilege of spending the best part of an hour, occasionally more, interviewing (almost) all of them in turn, to figure out precisely that – and what they may have in common.

Looking for commonalities may have been pointless. Beyond the fact that they have very nearly all enjoyed and practised writing in one form or another for a long time, often from an early age, their respective motivations are as varied as their personalities, backgrounds and occupations. They are academic researchers; full-time authors; journalists; consultants; authors "on the side" with a day job; working in the tech industry or in tech jobs (quite a few of them); in the civil service; in the humanitarian sector; in e-commerce.

Why do they write near-future science fiction, like they did for the Tales from the Cybersalon? Well, they did not all write stories that were strictly speaking near-future fictions, despite the framing of the calls. Some developed stories situated in realities alternate-but-similar-enough to ours. Some wrote fables for our times. Some stepped into a speculated near-future to explore its possible history, and our present in the process. But overall, they complied with the near-future fiction frame. Near-future science fiction is about stretching out a bit what is already there in a nascent or early development state; it is about picking threads in the present, which may seem unrelated, weaving them together in a "what would happen if?" kind of scenario and speculating as to how it may unfold.

Technology plays an important role in the stories, but not in a black-and-white kind of way. Interviewing the authors, I have found much ambivalence towards technology. Visions of beneficial, neutral as well as harmful technology; of technological determinism driving the world. Fascination, wonder and excitement, alongside anxiety, distrust, guilt even. Techno-solutionist hopes. Curiosity for the messy encounters between people and technology. Feelings of healthy scepticism, of helplessness, of horror at systems going out-of-control in the hands of (very human) rogue ambitions. All of these have fed into the stories.

Inspiration, again, has come from many places: from quirks and irks in the authors' day jobs; from emotionally intense personal life experience (infuriating, anxiogenic, baffling, moving, nostalgic); from existential questions close to their hearts; from the resonance between current preoccupations, trending issues and anecdotic stories in the news.

I asked the authors about their aims in creating and sharing short fictions with the Tales from the Cybersalon. For some, entertaining came first. Others prioritised delivering a message or making people think about the future – and the present – in other ways. But even if they placed the cursor differently between the two poles of entertainment and utility, they agreed on the necessity, and difficulty, of finding a balance between the two. Further, I found that short fictions can allow academic researchers to follow personal research interests through other means – another way of researching, teaching, and engaging with different audiences. Technologists can use it as an outlet for the emotional surplus and ethical questioning accumulated in their work.

Where do these disparate findings leave my attempt at tying together the authors in this volume, beyond the stories they have contributed?

Many of them like writing short fiction to calls, for the challenge, for the stimulation, for working to a deadline. But the Tales from the Cybersalon's calls were unusual in that they were about much more than writing a near-future science fiction short and releasing it into the world. The authors were to read their stories in public (even if online), to engage over their stories with a panel of experts and then with a live audience. But that is precisely what the authors relished overall: the engagement, with the panellists, with the public. Not trusting their words to an ocean of noise, at the mercy of serendipitous encounters with unknowable readers today, next month or many years from now, which, as an author pointed out, defeats much of the purpose of near-future sci-fi shorts by working on an utterly different timescale. Instead, they enjoyed the unique experience of immediate, interactive, informed responses to their writing. Above all, the authors relished their exchanges with the panellists, and if anything, would have liked a longer exposure to the "experts'" knowledgeable insights and perspectives. Several also appreciated the amount and quality of the research material provided – the luxury of having access to well-curated background research, on top of live expert knowledge. The Tales from the Cybersalon events were special in the level of engagement they demanded from the authors, but the authors loved it: newcomers and returners alike are up for more.

It is a truism that writing is a solitary experience, but the authors in this volume put the lie to it, who have woven their writings in a wider web of live interpersonal exchanges and found it enticing.

Do I have a more profound commonality to propose? Maybe.

These authors care. They care for us, for the future of us, and for a more-than-human future on Earth. Asked what writing near-future fiction brought her that academic writing did not, a researcher-*cum*-author commented that, "Being able to speculate is something that you are not necessarily allowed in academic work, for obvious reasons, but which I think has a lot of potential. It is quite useful to do, to open up the mind not only to what we have at the moment, but also to what could actually be."

I write from the perspective of a social scientist concerned with the social and ethical imports of future and emerging technologies, and I have the irritating habit of dragging things back to my vested interests. From my situated perspective, I propose that through their speculative fictions, the authors are engaging with us to develop an ethics of the future – a fundamentally relational, speculative ethics of the future, which, to borrow from a foundational paper theorising responsible innovation, would aim at "taking care of the future through collective stewardship of science and innovation in the present."[3]

Like the authors in this volume who write to try and make you think differently about the future, so have I about their stories, in the hope that you go back to them and read them… differently. That you share them, talk about them, find new uses for them, thus breathing life into thoughts they have tickled from their slumber.

---

3 Jack Stilgoe, Richard Owen, Phil Macnaghten. 2013. Developing a framework for responsible innovation. Research Policy 42(9): 1568-1580. DOI: https://doi.org/10.1016/j.respol.2013.05.008

About the Contributors

Cybersalon, digital think tank was founded at Networked Futures in 1997, just after third-party cookies had been legalised. We are a group of technologists, game designers, digital artists and academics, working on the edge of the future, building new solutions, researching and educating wide audiences about the threat of humans losing their agency in a data-driven society. We are affiliated to Middlesex and Westminster Universities and presented our proposals for a Bill of Digital Rights to the House of Commons in 2014-2015. Since 1997 Cybersalon has run over one hundred and twenty events on topics related to data in society, with large public consultations on digital rights, as well as writing the new EU digital skills course DigiBlox.org in 2019-2021.

Dr Christine Aicardi is a Senior Research Fellow in Science and Technology Studies at King's College London, having originally trained as an engineer working in the ICT industry. She has extensive experience collaborating with interdisciplinary teams to facilitate responsible research and innovation practices in computational neuroscience, brain-inspired computing and neurotechnology projects. Her research interests are the sciences and technologies of brain and mind; the study of interdisciplinary practices and collaborations; futures studies, notably the use of speculative science fiction for participatory foresight work.

Author (The Gray's Anatomy, Origamy, Invisible Ecologies and Soul Chasers: The Decomposition Comedy), Senior TED Fellow, and Professor of Regenerative Architecture at the Catholic University of Leuven (KU Leuven) Belgium, **Rachel Armstrong**, researches the inner life of "things" seen and unseen and experiments with the very stuff of life to ask how we may design and build our world differently.

Peter Baran is a mathematician, philosopher, and film historian who is interested in how technological advances, and other unforeseen events, inadvertently change society and art. A life-long Londoner, he has worked in education for over twenty years. He has written extensively online about film and popular culture as co-editor of www.freakytrigger.com. *Friday Night at The Horse and Zoom* is his first piece of published fiction.

David G.W. Birch is an author, advisor and commentator on digital financial services. An internationally-recognised thought leader in digital identity and digital money, he holds a number of board and advisory roles across these fields. He is a Forbes contributor and a columnist for Financial World. Previously named one of the global top fifteen favourite sources of business information by Wired magazine, he was identified as one of the top ten most influential voices in banking by Financial Brand.

Paul Currion works as a consultant for humanitarian organisations. His short fiction has been published by The White Review, Nature, Carve, Going Down Swinging and other magazines; and in anthologies for Virtual Futures, Fox Spirit, Leaf Books, and National Flash Fiction Day. His non-fiction has been published by Granta, Aeon, The Daily Telegraph and other magazines, and he has presented installations at the Vienna Biennale, Berlin Soundout!, and TransEuropa Belgrade. His website is www.currion.net.

Inventor and technology consultant **Angus Fraser** is an Agile Development Sherpa for Slalom, working with Amazon Air, Microsoft, and Salesforce partners. He has pioneered prototypes for ocean-rescue drones, ethical use of AI in Face Masks compliance, deploying facial recognition, and introduced Covid security e-monitoring in educational settings. Working with both hardware and software, Angus can usually be found on the cutting edge of new tech implementing pioneering devices. He is an ex-RAF pilot and loves tinkering with vintage planes and aero-acrobatics.

Benjamin Greenaway is a web applications developer, educator and ecommerce manager, with clients ranging from The Big Issue to the British Library. He recently contributed to the curriculum of a suite of digital media qualifications using the European Credit Transfer System and is currently Senior Web Development Manager at The Fold London. He occasionally writes non-fiction about technology, gaming and the web for online journals and industry magazines but his stories in this collection are his first published fiction.

Wendy M. Grossman is a freelance writer who specializes in computers, freedom, and privacy. Her work has appeared in the Guardian, New Scientist, Scientific American, and Wired. She also has a shady past as a travelling folksinger. Her website is at https://www.pelicancrossing.net.

David Gullen has sold over forty short stories to various magazines, anthologies and podcasts. Warm Gun won the BFS Short Story Competition in 2016, with other work short-listed for the James White Award and placed in the Aeon Award. David was born in Africa and baptised by King Neptune. He has lived in England most of his life and been telling stories for as long as he can remember. Find out more at www.davidgullen.com.

Liam Hogan is an award-winning short-story writer, with stories in Best of British Science Fiction and Best of British Fantasy (NewCon Press). He's been published by Analog, Daily Science Fiction, and Flame Tree Press, among others. He helps host Liars' League London, volunteers at the creative writing charity Ministry of Stories, and lives and avoids work in London. More details at http://happyendingnotguaranteed.blogspot.co.uk

Mark Huntley-James writes fantasy, science-fiction, or anything else that catches his attention. He has published three humorous urban fantasy novels, won the British Fantasy Society short story competition in 2013, and has various short and flash fiction in anthologies. He lives on a small farm with his partner, multiple cats, psycho-chickens, and rare-breed sheep. Sometimes he writes about the animals, but can't get any of them to read the stories. https://markhuntleyjames.wordpress.com

George Jacobs is a short-story writer of the fantastic and horrific. He has contributed to a number of anthologies and webzines, including Railroad Tales and Enchanted Conversation. George has worked in various fields, from oil & gas to planetary science, and now plans train schedules. He lives in the UK with his pet degus. https://georgejacobsauthor.wordpress.com/

Jane Norris writes speculative design fiction about our relationship to the objects and materials around us. She recently completed post-doc research in Critical Writing at the Royal College of Art. She has several published short stories, and has written a regular Dictionary of Craft column in the Crafts Council *CRAFTS* magazine and opinion pieces for the design magazine *Fiera*. She is an Associate Dean at Richmond University, the American University in London. Contact: @janeviatopia

Yen Ooi is a writer-researcher whose works explore East and Southeast Asian culture, identity and values. A PhD candidate at Royal Holloway, University of London and author of *Rén: The Ancient Chinese Art of Finding Peace and Fulfilment,* Yen writes fiction, non-fiction, poetry, and computer games. Yen co-edits Ab Terra, Brain Mill Press's science fiction imprint. When she hasn't got her head in a book, Yen also lectures, mentors, and plays the viola. www.yenooi.com

Stephen Oram writes near-future fiction which has been praised by publications as diverse as The Morning Star and The Financial Times. He works with artists, scientists, and technologists to explore possible future outcomes of their research through short stories and is a writer for sci-fi prototypers SciFutures. He is published in several anthologies and magazines, has two published novels and two collections of sci-fi shorts. www.stephenoram.net

Jule Owen was born and raised in the North of England. Jule has spent many years working in technology businesses and is fascinated by science, technology, and thinking about the future. Her five published novels and short stories are her creative response to the exponential growth of technological innovation in the era of climate change, with a bit of magic thrown in.

Eva Pascoe is a co-founder of the first Internet Café, "Cyberia", (London mid 1990s). She has set up the first TopShop online store and is currently Ecommerce Director at The Retail Practice. Since 2014 Eva has been involved with emerging Web3 infrastructure start-ups, campaigning for the use of hydropower for crypto mining. A consultant on an eco-friendly crypto accelerator in London, Eva is also an investor in women-led companies in sustainable tech and consumer goods. She is a winner of the Sunday Times Business Awards and has appeared on Newsnight and BBC Question Time. She writes short stories on the future of the high street, crypto and post-truth Internet. Eva is co-founder and chair of Cybersalon.

Jesse Rowell's background in technology, English literature and poetry informs the stories he writes. He has worked in multiple technology sectors including broadcast news monitoring, supply chain logistics, and software as a service (SaaS). His novels and short stories gravitate toward picaresque themes and dystopian settings. Jesse has been featured in multiple publications across media outlets, including NPR and several literary journals. https://jesserowell.com/

Douglas Rushkoff was named one of the "world's ten most influential intellectuals" by MIT. He is an author and documentarian who studies human autonomy in a digital age. He coined such concepts as "viral media", "screenagers", and "social currency", and has been a leading voice for applying digital media toward social and economic justice. The Media Ecology Association honored him with the first Neil Postman Award for Career Achievement in Public Intellectual Activity.

Britta Schulte writes. From one-line dystopias to PhD theses, they create technologies that we might get, to ask if we really want them. Sometimes they might create utopias. Or fairytales. Stories are spread over the Internet @brifrischu, self-published zines and selected anthologies.

Sophie Sparham is a poet and writer from Derby. She has written commissions for BBC Radio 4, The V&A and The People's History Museum. She co-hosts the night "Word Wise," which won best spoken word night at the 2019 Saboteur Awards. Her latest collection "The Man Who Ate 50,000 Weetabix" came out in April 2021 via Verve Poetry Press. Sophie's work has been published in Orbis, Under the Radar and The Morning Star. Her poem Sunrise Over Aldi won third place in the 2020 Charles Causley International Poetry Competition.

Having trained as an astronomer and subsequently managed a wide range of research projects in industry, **Vaughan Stanger** now writes SF and fantasy fiction full-time. His short stories have appeared in Nature Futures, Interzone, Daily Science Fiction, Abyss & Apex, and Sci Phi Journal, among others. His most recent collection is The Last Moonshot & Other Stories. Follow his writing adventures at http://www.vaughanstanger.com or @ VaughanStanger.

Acknowledgements

We would like to say a big thank you to all those who contributed to the *Tales from the Cybersalon* events which formed the basis of this book.

Specifically, the expert panellists: Dr Christine Aicardi, Professor Rachel Armstrong, David G.W. Birch, Angus Fraser, Professor Lucy Hooberman, Jana Hlistova, Caron Lyon, Yen Ooi, Priya Prakesh, Edward Saperia, Simon Sarginson, and Paul Wilson.

Finally, we would like to acknowledge the contribution of the audiences who listened intently to the stories and to the experts, and asked the pertinent questions.

CPSIA information can be obtained
at www.ICGtesting.com
Printed in the USA
LVHW092006191122
733499LV00019B/1483